C-2942 CAREER EXAMINATION SERIES

This is your
PASSBOOK for...

Park Maintenance Supervisor

Test Preparation Study Guide
Questions & Answers

COPYRIGHT NOTICE

This book is SOLELY intended for, is sold ONLY to, and its use is RESTRICTED to individual, bona fide applicants or candidates who qualify by virtue of having seriously filed applications for appropriate license, certificate, professional and/or promotional advancement, higher school matriculation, scholarship, or other legitimate requirements of education and/or governmental authorities.

This book is NOT intended for use, class instruction, tutoring, training, duplication, copying, reprinting, excerption, or adaptation, etc., by:

1) Other publishers
2) Proprietors and/or Instructors of "Coaching" and/or Preparatory Courses
3) Personnel and/or Training Divisions of commercial, industrial, and governmental organizations
4) Schools, colleges, or universities and/or their departments and staffs, including teachers and other personnel
5) Testing Agencies or Bureaus
6) Study groups which seek by the purchase of a single volume to copy and/or duplicate and/or adapt this material for use by the group as a whole without having purchased individual volumes for each of the members of the group
7) Et al.

Such persons would be in violation of appropriate Federal and State statutes.

PROVISION OF LICENSING AGREEMENTS – Recognized educational, commercial, industrial, and governmental institutions and organizations, and others legitimately engaged in educational pursuits, including training, testing, and measurement activities, may address request for a licensing agreement to the copyright owners, who will determine whether, and under what conditions, including fees and charges, the materials in this book may be used them. In other words, a licensing facility exists for the legitimate use of the material in this book on other than an individual basis. However, it is asseverated and affirmed here that the material in this book CANNOT be used without the receipt of the express permission of such a licensing agreement from the Publishers. Inquiries re licensing should be addressed to the company, attention rights and permissions department.

All rights reserved, including the right of reproduction in whole or in part, in any form or by any means, electronic or mechanical, including photocopying, recording, or by any information storage and retrieval system, without permission in writing from the Publisher.

Copyright © 2024 by
National Learning Corporation

212 Michael Drive, Syosset, NY 11791
(516) 921-8888 • www.passbooks.com
E-mail: info@passbooks.com

PUBLISHED IN THE UNITED STATES OF AMERICA

PASSBOOK® SERIES

THE *PASSBOOK® SERIES* has been created to prepare applicants and candidates for the ultimate academic battlefield – the examination room.

At some time in our lives, each and every one of us may be required to take an examination – for validation, matriculation, admission, qualification, registration, certification, or licensure.

Based on the assumption that every applicant or candidate has met the basic formal educational standards, has taken the required number of courses, and read the necessary texts, the *PASSBOOK® SERIES* furnishes the one special preparation which may assure passing with confidence, instead of failing with insecurity. Examination questions – together with answers – are furnished as the basic vehicle for study so that the mysteries of the examination and its compounding difficulties may be eliminated or diminished by a sure method.

This book is meant to help you pass your examination provided that you qualify and are serious in your objective.

The entire field is reviewed through the huge store of content information which is succinctly presented through a provocative and challenging approach – the question-and-answer method.

A climate of success is established by furnishing the correct answers at the end of each test.

You soon learn to recognize types of questions, forms of questions, and patterns of questioning. You may even begin to anticipate expected outcomes.

You perceive that many questions are repeated or adapted so that you can gain acute insights, which may enable you to score many sure points.

You learn how to confront new questions, or types of questions, and to attack them confidently and work out the correct answers.

You note objectives and emphases, and recognize pitfalls and dangers, so that you may make positive educational adjustments.

Moreover, you are kept fully informed in relation to new concepts, methods, practices, and directions in the field.

You discover that you are actually taking the examination all the time: you are preparing for the examination by "taking" an examination, not by reading extraneous and/or supererogatory textbooks.

In short, this PASSBOOK®, used directedly, should be an important factor in helping you to pass your test.

PARKS MAINTENANCE SUPERVISOR

DUTIES:
 Plans, organizes, assigns, and supervises maintenance activities in parks and recreational areas. Performs related duties as required.

SCOPE OF THE EXAMINATION:
The written test will be designed to test for knowledge, skills, and/or abilities in such areas as:

1. **Administrative Supervision** -These questions test for knowledge of the principles and practices involved in directing the activities of a large subordinate staff, including subordinate supervisors. Questions relate to the personal interactions between an upper level supervisor and his/her subordinate supervisors in the accomplishment of objectives. These questions cover such areas as assigning work to and coordinating the activities of several units, establishing and guiding staff development programs, evaluating the performance of subordinate supervisors, and maintaining relationships with other organizational sections.
2. **Administrative Techniques and Practices** - These questions test for a knowledge of management techniques and practices used in directing or assisting in directing a program component or an organizational segment. Questions cover such areas as interpreting, policies, making decisions based on the context of the position in the organization, coordinating programs or projects, communicating with employees or the public, planning employee training, and researching and evaluating areas of concern.
3. **Grounds Maintenance, including Turf, Trees and Shrubs** - These questions test for knowledge of the principles and practices involved in grounds maintenance and may include such areas as turf grass planting, fertilizing, and maintenance; tree and shrub selection, planting, transplanting, trimming and maintenance; snow and ice control; and safe operating practices involved when performing grounds maintenance activities.
4. **Maintenance of Buildings and Equipment** - These questions test for knowledge of the principles and. practices involved in the overall maintenance, construction, and upkeep of the typical structures, buildings, and equipment found in park facilities; arid may include such areas as proper maintenance and repair of buildings, roadways, trails, flood control and drainage structures, minor mechanical and electrical systems maintenance, and safe operating practices.
5. **Installation, Maintenance, and Repair of Recreation Areas** - These questions test for knowledge of the principles and practices involved in the installation, upkeep, maintenance and repair of park and recreation facilities, including such areas as picnic facilities, playgrounds, athletic and playing fields, trails and walkways. sanitary facilities, and lawn care and grounds maintenance,
6. **Preparing Written Material** - These questions test for the ability to present information clearly and accurately, and to organize paragraphs logically and comprehensibly. For some questions, you will be given information in two or three sentences followed by four restatements of the information. You must then choose the best version. For other questions, you will be given paragraphs with their sentences out of order. You must then choose, from four suggestions, the best order for the sentences.

HOW TO TAKE A TEST

I. YOU MUST PASS AN EXAMINATION

A. WHAT EVERY CANDIDATE SHOULD KNOW

Examination applicants often ask us for help in preparing for the written test. What can I study in advance? What kinds of questions will be asked? How will the test be given? How will the papers be graded?

As an applicant for a civil service examination, you may be wondering about some of these things. Our purpose here is to suggest effective methods of advance study and to describe civil service examinations.

Your chances for success on this examination can be increased if you know how to prepare. Those "pre-examination jitters" can be reduced if you know what to expect. You can even experience an adventure in good citizenship if you know why civil service exams are given.

B. WHY ARE CIVIL SERVICE EXAMINATIONS GIVEN?

Civil service examinations are important to you in two ways. As a citizen, you want public jobs filled by employees who know how to do their work. As a job seeker, you want a fair chance to compete for that job on an equal footing with other candidates. The best-known means of accomplishing this two-fold goal is the competitive examination.

Exams are widely publicized throughout the nation. They may be administered for jobs in federal, state, city, municipal, town or village governments or agencies.

Any citizen may apply, with some limitations, such as the age or residence of applicants. Your experience and education may be reviewed to see whether you meet the requirements for the particular examination. When these requirements exist, they are reasonable and applied consistently to all applicants. Thus, a competitive examination may cause you some uneasiness now, but it is your privilege and safeguard.

C. HOW ARE CIVIL SERVICE EXAMS DEVELOPED?

Examinations are carefully written by trained technicians who are specialists in the field known as "psychological measurement," in consultation with recognized authorities in the field of work that the test will cover. These experts recommend the subject matter areas or skills to be tested; only those knowledges or skills important to your success on the job are included. The most reliable books and source materials available are used as references. Together, the experts and technicians judge the difficulty level of the questions.

Test technicians know how to phrase questions so that the problem is clearly stated. Their ethics do not permit "trick" or "catch" questions. Questions may have been tried out on sample groups, or subjected to statistical analysis, to determine their usefulness.

Written tests are often used in combination with performance tests, ratings of training and experience, and oral interviews. All of these measures combine to form the best-known means of finding the right person for the right job.

II. HOW TO PASS THE WRITTEN TEST

A. NATURE OF THE EXAMINATION

To prepare intelligently for civil service examinations, you should know how they differ from school examinations you have taken. In school you were assigned certain definite pages to read or subjects to cover. The examination questions were quite detailed and usually emphasized memory. Civil service exams, on the other hand, try to discover your present ability to perform the duties of a position, plus your potentiality to learn these duties. In other words, a civil service exam attempts to predict how successful you will be. Questions cover such a broad area that they cannot be as minute and detailed as school exam questions.

In the public service similar kinds of work, or positions, are grouped together in one "class." This process is known as *position-classification*. All the positions in a class are paid according to the salary range for that class. One class title covers all of these positions, and they are all tested by the same examination.

B. FOUR BASIC STEPS

1) Study the announcement

How, then, can you know what subjects to study? Our best answer is: "Learn as much as possible about the class of positions for which you've applied." The exam will test the knowledge, skills and abilities needed to do the work.

Your most valuable source of information about the position you want is the official exam announcement. This announcement lists the training and experience qualifications. Check these standards and apply only if you come reasonably close to meeting them.

The brief description of the position in the examination announcement offers some clues to the subjects which will be tested. Think about the job itself. Review the duties in your mind. Can you perform them, or are there some in which you are rusty? Fill in the blank spots in your preparation.

Many jurisdictions preview the written test in the exam announcement by including a section called "Knowledge and Abilities Required," "Scope of the Examination," or some similar heading. Here you will find out specifically what fields will be tested.

2) Review your own background

Once you learn in general what the position is all about, and what you need to know to do the work, ask yourself which subjects you already know fairly well and which need improvement. You may wonder whether to concentrate on improving your strong areas or on building some background in your fields of weakness. When the announcement has specified "some knowledge" or "considerable knowledge," or has used adjectives like "beginning principles of…" or "advanced … methods," you can get a clue as to the number and difficulty of questions to be asked in any given field. More questions, and hence broader coverage, would be included for those subjects which are more important in the work. Now weigh your strengths and weaknesses against the job requirements and prepare accordingly.

3) Determine the level of the position

Another way to tell how intensively you should prepare is to understand the level of the job for which you are applying. Is it the entering level? In other words, is this the position in which beginners in a field of work are hired? Or is it an intermediate or advanced level? Sometimes this is indicated by such words as "Junior" or "Senior" in the class title. Other jurisdictions use Roman numerals to designate the level – Clerk I, Clerk II, for example. The word "Supervisor" sometimes appears in the title. If the level is not indicated by the title, check the description of duties. Will you be working under very close supervision, or will you have responsibility for independent decisions in this work?

4) Choose appropriate study materials

Now that you know the subjects to be examined and the relative amount of each subject to be covered, you can choose suitable study materials. For beginning level jobs, or even advanced ones, if you have a pronounced weakness in some aspect of your training, read a modern, standard textbook in that field. Be sure it is up to date and has general coverage. Such books are normally available at your library, and the librarian will be glad to help you locate one. For entry-level positions, questions of appropriate difficulty are chosen – neither highly advanced questions, nor those too simple. Such questions require careful thought but not advanced training.

If the position for which you are applying is technical or advanced, you will read more advanced, specialized material. If you are already familiar with the basic principles of your field, elementary textbooks would waste your time. Concentrate on advanced textbooks and technical periodicals. Think through the concepts and review difficult problems in your field.

These are all general sources. You can get more ideas on your own initiative, following these leads. For example, training manuals and publications of the government agency which employs workers in your field can be useful, particularly for technical and professional positions. A letter or visit to the government department involved may result in more specific study suggestions, and certainly will provide you with a more definite idea of the exact nature of the position you are seeking.

III. KINDS OF TESTS

Tests are used for purposes other than measuring knowledge and ability to perform specified duties. For some positions, it is equally important to test ability to make adjustments to new situations or to profit from training. In others, basic mental abilities not dependent on information are essential. Questions which test these things may not appear as pertinent to the duties of the position as those which test for knowledge and information. Yet they are often highly important parts of a fair examination. For very general questions, it is almost impossible to help you direct your study efforts. What we can do is to point out some of the more common of these general abilities needed in public service positions and describe some typical questions.

1) General information

Broad, general information has been found useful for predicting job success in some kinds of work. This is tested in a variety of ways, from vocabulary lists to questions about current events. Basic background in some field of work, such as sociology or economics, may be sampled in a group of questions. Often these are principles which have become familiar to most persons through exposure rather than through formal training. It is difficult to advise you how to study for these questions; being alert to the world around you is our best suggestion.

2) Verbal ability

An example of an ability needed in many positions is verbal or language ability. Verbal ability is, in brief, the ability to use and understand words. Vocabulary and grammar tests are typical measures of this ability. Reading comprehension or paragraph interpretation questions are common in many kinds of civil service tests. You are given a paragraph of written material and asked to find its central meaning.

3) **Numerical ability**

Number skills can be tested by the familiar arithmetic problem, by checking paired lists of numbers to see which are alike and which are different, or by interpreting charts and graphs. In the latter test, a graph may be printed in the test booklet which you are asked to use as the basis for answering questions.

4) **Observation**

A popular test for law-enforcement positions is the observation test. A picture is shown to you for several minutes, then taken away. Questions about the picture test your ability to observe both details and larger elements.

5) **Following directions**

In many positions in the public service, the employee must be able to carry out written instructions dependably and accurately. You may be given a chart with several columns, each column listing a variety of information. The questions require you to carry out directions involving the information given in the chart.

6) **Skills and aptitudes**

Performance tests effectively measure some manual skills and aptitudes. When the skill is one in which you are trained, such as typing or shorthand, you can practice. These tests are often very much like those given in business school or high school courses. For many of the other skills and aptitudes, however, no short-time preparation can be made. Skills and abilities natural to you or that you have developed throughout your lifetime are being tested.

Many of the general questions just described provide all the data needed to answer the questions and ask you to use your reasoning ability to find the answers. Your best preparation for these tests, as well as for tests of facts and ideas, is to be at your physical and mental best. You, no doubt, have your own methods of getting into an exam-taking mood and keeping "in shape." The next section lists some ideas on this subject.

IV. KINDS OF QUESTIONS

Only rarely is the "essay" question, which you answer in narrative form, used in civil service tests. Civil service tests are usually of the short-answer type. Full instructions for answering these questions will be given to you at the examination. But in case this is your first experience with short-answer questions and separate answer sheets, here is what you need to know:

1) Multiple-choice Questions

Most popular of the short-answer questions is the "multiple choice" or "best answer" question. It can be used, for example, to test for factual knowledge, ability to solve problems or judgment in meeting situations found at work.

A multiple-choice question is normally one of three types—
- It can begin with an incomplete statement followed by several possible endings. You are to find the one ending which *best* completes the statement, although some of the others may not be entirely wrong.
- It can also be a complete statement in the form of a question which is answered by choosing one of the statements listed.

- It can be in the form of a problem – again you select the best answer.

Here is an example of a multiple-choice question with a discussion which should give you some clues as to the method for choosing the right answer:

When an employee has a complaint about his assignment, the action which will *best* help him overcome his difficulty is to
   A. discuss his difficulty with his coworkers
   B. take the problem to the head of the organization
   C. take the problem to the person who gave him the assignment
   D. say nothing to anyone about his complaint

In answering this question, you should study each of the choices to find which is best. Consider choice "A" – Certainly an employee may discuss his complaint with fellow employees, but no change or improvement can result, and the complaint remains unresolved. Choice "B" is a poor choice since the head of the organization probably does not know what assignment you have been given, and taking your problem to him is known as "going over the head" of the supervisor. The supervisor, or person who made the assignment, is the person who can clarify it or correct any injustice. Choice "C" is, therefore, correct. To say nothing, as in choice "D," is unwise. Supervisors have and interest in knowing the problems employees are facing, and the employee is seeking a solution to his problem.

2) True/False Questions

The "true/false" or "right/wrong" form of question is sometimes used. Here a complete statement is given. Your job is to decide whether the statement is right or wrong.

SAMPLE: A roaming cell-phone call to a nearby city costs less than a non-roaming call to a distant city.

This statement is wrong, or false, since roaming calls are more expensive.

This is not a complete list of all possible question forms, although most of the others are variations of these common types. You will always get complete directions for answering questions. Be sure you understand *how* to mark your answers – ask questions until you do.

V. RECORDING YOUR ANSWERS

Computer terminals are used more and more today for many different kinds of exams.
For an examination with very few applicants, you may be told to record your answers in the test booklet itself. Separate answer sheets are much more common. If this separate answer sheet is to be scored by machine – and this is often the case – it is highly important that you mark your answers correctly in order to get credit.
An electronic scoring machine is often used in civil service offices because of the speed with which papers can be scored. Machine-scored answer sheets must be marked with a pencil, which will be given to you. This pencil has a high graphite content which responds to the electronic scoring machine. As a matter of fact, stray dots may register as answers, so do not let your pencil rest on the answer sheet while you are pondering the correct answer. Also, if your pencil lead breaks or is otherwise defective, ask for another.

Since the answer sheet will be dropped in a slot in the scoring machine, be careful not to bend the corners or get the paper crumpled.

The answer sheet normally has five vertical columns of numbers, with 30 numbers to a column. These numbers correspond to the question numbers in your test booklet. After each number, going across the page are four or five pairs of dotted lines. These short dotted lines have small letters or numbers above them. The first two pairs may also have a "T" or "F" above the letters. This indicates that the first two pairs only are to be used if the questions are of the true-false type. If the questions are multiple choice, disregard the "T" and "F" and pay attention only to the small letters or numbers.

Answer your questions in the manner of the sample that follows:

32. The largest city in the United States is
    A. Washington, D.C.
    B. New York City
    C. Chicago
    D. Detroit
    E. San Francisco

1) Choose the answer you think is best. (New York City is the largest, so "B" is correct.)
2) Find the row of dotted lines numbered the same as the question you are answering. (Find row number 32)
3) Find the pair of dotted lines corresponding to the answer. (Find the pair of lines under the mark "B.")
4) Make a solid black mark between the dotted lines.

VI. BEFORE THE TEST

Common sense will help you find procedures to follow to get ready for an examination. Too many of us, however, overlook these sensible measures. Indeed, nervousness and fatigue have been found to be the most serious reasons why applicants fail to do their best on civil service tests. Here is a list of reminders:

- Begin your preparation early – Don't wait until the last minute to go scurrying around for books and materials or to find out what the position is all about.
- Prepare continuously – An hour a night for a week is better than an all-night cram session. This has been definitely established. What is more, a night a week for a month will return better dividends than crowding your study into a shorter period of time.
- Locate the place of the exam – You have been sent a notice telling you when and where to report for the examination. If the location is in a different town or otherwise unfamiliar to you, it would be well to inquire the best route and learn something about the building.
- Relax the night before the test – Allow your mind to rest. Do not study at all that night. Plan some mild recreation or diversion; then go to bed early and get a good night's sleep.
- Get up early enough to make a leisurely trip to the place for the test – This way unforeseen events, traffic snarls, unfamiliar buildings, etc. will not upset you.
- Dress comfortably – A written test is not a fashion show. You will be known by number and not by name, so wear something comfortable.

- Leave excess paraphernalia at home – Shopping bags and odd bundles will get in your way. You need bring only the items mentioned in the official notice you received; usually everything you need is provided. Do not bring reference books to the exam. They will only confuse those last minutes and be taken away from you when in the test room.
- Arrive somewhat ahead of time – If because of transportation schedules you must get there very early, bring a newspaper or magazine to take your mind off yourself while waiting.
- Locate the examination room – When you have found the proper room, you will be directed to the seat or part of the room where you will sit. Sometimes you are given a sheet of instructions to read while you are waiting. Do not fill out any forms until you are told to do so; just read them and be prepared.
- Relax and prepare to listen to the instructions
- If you have any physical problem that may keep you from doing your best, be sure to tell the test administrator. If you are sick or in poor health, you really cannot do your best on the exam. You can come back and take the test some other time.

VII. AT THE TEST

The day of the test is here and you have the test booklet in your hand. The temptation to get going is very strong. Caution! There is more to success than knowing the right answers. You must know how to identify your papers and understand variations in the type of short-answer question used in this particular examination. Follow these suggestions for maximum results from your efforts:

1) Cooperate with the monitor

The test administrator has a duty to create a situation in which you can be as much at ease as possible. He will give instructions, tell you when to begin, check to see that you are marking your answer sheet correctly, and so on. He is not there to guard you, although he will see that your competitors do not take unfair advantage. He wants to help you do your best.

2) Listen to all instructions

Don't jump the gun! Wait until you understand all directions. In most civil service tests you get more time than you need to answer the questions. So don't be in a hurry. Read each word of instructions until you clearly understand the meaning. Study the examples, listen to all announcements and follow directions. Ask questions if you do not understand what to do.

3) Identify your papers

Civil service exams are usually identified by number only. You will be assigned a number; you must not put your name on your test papers. Be sure to copy your number correctly. Since more than one exam may be given, copy your exact examination title.

4) Plan your time

Unless you are told that a test is a "speed" or "rate of work" test, speed itself is usually not important. Time enough to answer all the questions will be provided, but this does not mean that you have all day. An overall time limit has been set. Divide the total time (in minutes) by the number of questions to determine the approximate time you have for each question.

5) Do not linger over difficult questions

If you come across a difficult question, mark it with a paper clip (useful to have along) and come back to it when you have been through the booklet. One caution if you do this – be sure to skip a number on your answer sheet as well. Check often to be sure that you have not lost your place and that you are marking in the row numbered the same as the question you are answering.

6) Read the questions

Be sure you know what the question asks! Many capable people are unsuccessful because they failed to *read* the questions correctly.

7) Answer all questions

Unless you have been instructed that a penalty will be deducted for incorrect answers, it is better to guess than to omit a question.

8) Speed tests

It is often better NOT to guess on speed tests. It has been found that on timed tests people are tempted to spend the last few seconds before time is called in marking answers at random – without even reading them – in the hope of picking up a few extra points. To discourage this practice, the instructions may warn you that your score will be "corrected" for guessing. That is, a penalty will be applied. The incorrect answers will be deducted from the correct ones, or some other penalty formula will be used.

9) Review your answers

If you finish before time is called, go back to the questions you guessed or omitted to give them further thought. Review other answers if you have time.

10) Return your test materials

If you are ready to leave before others have finished or time is called, take ALL your materials to the monitor and leave quietly. Never take any test material with you. The monitor can discover whose papers are not complete, and taking a test booklet may be grounds for disqualification.

VIII. EXAMINATION TECHNIQUES

1) Read the general instructions carefully. These are usually printed on the first page of the exam booklet. As a rule, these instructions refer to the timing of the examination; the fact that you should not start work until the signal and must stop work at a signal, etc. If there are any *special* instructions, such as a choice of questions to be answered, make sure that you note this instruction carefully.

2) When you are ready to start work on the examination, that is as soon as the signal has been given, read the instructions to each question booklet, underline any key words or phrases, such as *least, best, outline, describe* and the like. In this way you will tend to answer as requested rather than discover on reviewing your paper that you *listed without describing*, that you selected the *worst* choice rather than the *best* choice, etc.

3) If the examination is of the objective or multiple-choice type – that is, each question will also give a series of possible answers: A, B, C or D, and you are called upon to select the best answer and write the letter next to that answer on your answer paper – it is advisable to start answering each question in turn. There may be anywhere from 50 to 100 such questions in the three or four hours allotted and you can see how much time would be taken if you read through all the questions before beginning to answer any. Furthermore, if you come across a question or group of questions which you know would be difficult to answer, it would undoubtedly affect your handling of all the other questions.

4) If the examination is of the essay type and contains but a few questions, it is a moot point as to whether you should read all the questions before starting to answer any one. Of course, if you are given a choice – say five out of seven and the like – then it is essential to read all the questions so you can eliminate the two that are most difficult. If, however, you are asked to answer all the questions, there may be danger in trying to answer the easiest one first because you may find that you will spend too much time on it. The best technique is to answer the first question, then proceed to the second, etc.

5) Time your answers. Before the exam begins, write down the time it started, then add the time allowed for the examination and write down the time it must be completed, then divide the time available somewhat as follows:
    - If 3-1/2 hours are allowed, that would be 210 minutes. If you have 80 objective-type questions, that would be an average of 2-1/2 minutes per question. Allow yourself no more than 2 minutes per question, or a total of 160 minutes, which will permit about 50 minutes to review.
    - If for the time allotment of 210 minutes there are 7 essay questions to answer, that would average about 30 minutes a question. Give yourself only 25 minutes per question so that you have about 35 minutes to review.

6) The most important instruction is to *read each question* and make sure you know what is wanted. The second most important instruction is to *time yourself properly* so that you answer every question. The third most important instruction is to *answer every question*. Guess if you have to but include something for each question. Remember that you will receive no credit for a blank and will probably receive some credit if you write something in answer to an essay question. If you guess a letter – say "B" for a multiple-choice question – you may have guessed right. If you leave a blank as an answer to a multiple-choice question, the examiners may respect your feelings but it will not add a point to your score. Some exams may penalize you for wrong answers, so in such cases *only*, you may not want to guess unless you have some basis for your answer.

7) Suggestions
    a. Objective-type questions
        1. Examine the question booklet for proper sequence of pages and questions
        2. Read all instructions carefully
        3. Skip any question which seems too difficult; return to it after all other questions have been answered
        4. Apportion your time properly; do not spend too much time on any single question or group of questions

5. Note and underline key words – *all, most, fewest, least, best, worst, same, opposite,* etc.
6. Pay particular attention to negatives
7. Note unusual option, e.g., unduly long, short, complex, different or similar in content to the body of the question
8. Observe the use of "hedging" words – *probably, may, most likely,* etc.
9. Make sure that your answer is put next to the same number as the question
10. Do not second-guess unless you have good reason to believe the second answer is definitely more correct
11. Cross out original answer if you decide another answer is more accurate; do not erase until you are ready to hand your paper in
12. Answer all questions; guess unless instructed otherwise
13. Leave time for review

  b. Essay questions
1. Read each question carefully
2. Determine exactly what is wanted. Underline key words or phrases.
3. Decide on outline or paragraph answer
4. Include many different points and elements unless asked to develop any one or two points or elements
5. Show impartiality by giving pros and cons unless directed to select one side only
6. Make and write down any assumptions you find necessary to answer the questions
7. Watch your English, grammar, punctuation and choice of words
8. Time your answers; don't crowd material

8) Answering the essay question

Most essay questions can be answered by framing the specific response around several key words or ideas. Here are a few such key words or ideas:

M's: manpower, materials, methods, money, management
P's: purpose, program, policy, plan, procedure, practice, problems, pitfalls, personnel, public relations

  a. Six basic steps in handling problems:
1. Preliminary plan and background development
2. Collect information, data and facts
3. Analyze and interpret information, data and facts
4. Analyze and develop solutions as well as make recommendations
5. Prepare report and sell recommendations
6. Install recommendations and follow up effectiveness

  b. Pitfalls to avoid
1. *Taking things for granted* – A statement of the situation does not necessarily imply that each of the elements is necessarily true; for example, a complaint may be invalid and biased so that all that can be taken for granted is that a complaint has been registered

2. *Considering only one side of a situation* – Wherever possible, indicate several alternatives and then point out the reasons you selected the best one
3. *Failing to indicate follow up* – Whenever your answer indicates action on your part, make certain that you will take proper follow-up action to see how successful your recommendations, procedures or actions turn out to be
4. *Taking too long in answering any single question* – Remember to time your answers properly

IX. AFTER THE TEST

Scoring procedures differ in detail among civil service jurisdictions although the general principles are the same. Whether the papers are hand-scored or graded by machine we have described, they are nearly always graded by number. That is, the person who marks the paper knows only the number – never the name – of the applicant. Not until all the papers have been graded will they be matched with names. If other tests, such as training and experience or oral interview ratings have been given, scores will be combined. Different parts of the examination usually have different weights. For example, the written test might count 60 percent of the final grade, and a rating of training and experience 40 percent. In many jurisdictions, veterans will have a certain number of points added to their grades.

After the final grade has been determined, the names are placed in grade order and an eligible list is established. There are various methods for resolving ties between those who get the same final grade – probably the most common is to place first the name of the person whose application was received first. Job offers are made from the eligible list in the order the names appear on it. You will be notified of your grade and your rank as soon as all these computations have been made. This will be done as rapidly as possible.

People who are found to meet the requirements in the announcement are called "eligibles." Their names are put on a list of eligible candidates. An eligible's chances of getting a job depend on how high he stands on this list and how fast agencies are filling jobs from the list.

When a job is to be filled from a list of eligibles, the agency asks for the names of people on the list of eligibles for that job. When the civil service commission receives this request, it sends to the agency the names of the three people highest on this list. Or, if the job to be filled has specialized requirements, the office sends the agency the names of the top three persons who meet these requirements from the general list.

The appointing officer makes a choice from among the three people whose names were sent to him. If the selected person accepts the appointment, the names of the others are put back on the list to be considered for future openings.

That is the rule in hiring from all kinds of eligible lists, whether they are for typist, carpenter, chemist, or something else. For every vacancy, the appointing officer has his choice of any one of the top three eligibles on the list. This explains why the person whose name is on top of the list sometimes does not get an appointment when some of the persons lower on the list do. If the appointing officer chooses the second or third eligible, the No. 1 eligible does not get a job at once, but stays on the list until he is appointed or the list is terminated.

X. HOW TO PASS THE INTERVIEW TEST

The examination for which you applied requires an oral interview test. You have already taken the written test and you are now being called for the interview test – the final part of the formal examination.

You may think that it is not possible to prepare for an interview test and that there are no procedures to follow during an interview. Our purpose is to point out some things you can do in advance that will help you and some good rules to follow and pitfalls to avoid while you are being interviewed.

What is an interview supposed to test?

The written examination is designed to test the technical knowledge and competence of the candidate; the oral is designed to evaluate intangible qualities, not readily measured otherwise, and to establish a list showing the relative fitness of each candidate – as measured against his competitors – for the position sought. Scoring is not on the basis of "right" and "wrong," but on a sliding scale of values ranging from "not passable" to "outstanding." As a matter of fact, it is possible to achieve a relatively low score without a single "incorrect" answer because of evident weakness in the qualities being measured.

Occasionally, an examination may consist entirely of an oral test – either an individual or a group oral. In such cases, information is sought concerning the technical knowledges and abilities of the candidate, since there has been no written examination for this purpose. More commonly, however, an oral test is used to supplement a written examination.

Who conducts interviews?

The composition of oral boards varies among different jurisdictions. In nearly all, a representative of the personnel department serves as chairman. One of the members of the board may be a representative of the department in which the candidate would work. In some cases, "outside experts" are used, and, frequently, a businessman or some other representative of the general public is asked to serve. Labor and management or other special groups may be represented. The aim is to secure the services of experts in the appropriate field.

However the board is composed, it is a good idea (and not at all improper or unethical) to ascertain in advance of the interview who the members are and what groups they represent. When you are introduced to them, you will have some idea of their backgrounds and interests, and at least you will not stutter and stammer over their names.

What should be done before the interview?

While knowledge about the board members is useful and takes some of the surprise element out of the interview, there is other preparation which is more substantive. It *is* possible to prepare for an oral interview – in several ways:

1) Keep a copy of your application and review it carefully before the interview

This may be the only document before the oral board, and the starting point of the interview. Know what education and experience you have listed there, and the sequence and dates of all of it. Sometimes the board will ask you to review the highlights of your experience for them; you should not have to hem and haw doing it.

2) Study the class specification and the examination announcement

Usually, the oral board has one or both of these to guide them. The qualities, characteristics or knowledges required by the position sought are stated in these documents. They offer valuable clues as to the nature of the oral interview. For example, if the job involves supervisory responsibilities, the announcement will usually indicate that knowledge of modern supervisory methods and the qualifications of the candidate as a supervisor will be tested. If so, you can expect such questions, frequently in the form of a hypothetical situation which you are expected to solve. NEVER go into an oral without knowledge of the duties and responsibilities of the job you seek.

3) Think through each qualification required

Try to visualize the kind of questions you would ask if you were a board member. How well could you answer them? Try especially to appraise your own knowledge and background in each area, *measured against the job sought*, and identify any areas in which you are weak. Be critical and realistic – do not flatter yourself.

4) Do some general reading in areas in which you feel you may be weak

For example, if the job involves supervision and your past experience has NOT, some general reading in supervisory methods and practices, particularly in the field of human relations, might be useful. Do NOT study agency procedures or detailed manuals. The oral board will be testing your understanding and capacity, not your memory.

5) Get a good night's sleep and watch your general health and mental attitude

You will want a clear head at the interview. Take care of a cold or any other minor ailment, and of course, no hangovers.

What should be done on the day of the interview?

Now comes the day of the interview itself. Give yourself plenty of time to get there. Plan to arrive somewhat ahead of the scheduled time, particularly if your appointment is in the fore part of the day. If a previous candidate fails to appear, the board might be ready for you a bit early. By early afternoon an oral board is almost invariably behind schedule if there are many candidates, and you may have to wait. Take along a book or magazine to read, or your application to review, but leave any extraneous material in the waiting room when you go in for your interview. In any event, relax and compose yourself.

The matter of dress is important. The board is forming impressions about you – from your experience, your manners, your attitude, and your appearance. Give your personal appearance careful attention. Dress your best, but not your flashiest. Choose conservative, appropriate clothing, and be sure it is immaculate. This is a business interview, and your appearance should indicate that you regard it as such. Besides, being well groomed and properly dressed will help boost your confidence.

Sooner or later, someone will call your name and escort you into the interview room. *This is it.* From here on you are on your own. It is too late for any more preparation. But remember, you asked for this opportunity to prove your fitness, and you are here because your request was granted.

What happens when you go in?

The usual sequence of events will be as follows: The clerk (who is often the board stenographer) will introduce you to the chairman of the oral board, who will introduce you to the other members of the board. Acknowledge the introductions before you sit down. Do not be surprised if you find a microphone facing you or a stenotypist sitting by. Oral interviews are usually recorded in the event of an appeal or other review.

Usually the chairman of the board will open the interview by reviewing the highlights of your education and work experience from your application – primarily for the benefit of the other members of the board, as well as to get the material into the record. Do not interrupt or comment unless there is an error or significant misinterpretation; if that is the case, do not hesitate. But do not quibble about insignificant matters. Also, he will usually ask you some question about your education, experience or your present job – partly to get you to start talking and to establish the interviewing "rapport." He may start the actual questioning, or turn it over to one of the other members. Frequently, each member undertakes the questioning on a particular area, one in which he is perhaps most competent, so you can expect each member to participate in the examination. Because time is limited, you may also expect some rather abrupt switches in the direction the questioning takes, so do not be upset by it. Normally, a board member will not pursue a single line of questioning unless he discovers a particular strength or weakness.

After each member has participated, the chairman will usually ask whether any member has any further questions, then will ask you if you have anything you wish to add. Unless you are expecting this question, it may floor you. Worse, it may start you off on an extended, extemporaneous speech. The board is not usually seeking more information. The question is principally to offer you a last opportunity to present further qualifications or to indicate that you have nothing to add. So, if you feel that a significant qualification or characteristic has been overlooked, it is proper to point it out in a sentence or so. Do not compliment the board on the thoroughness of their examination – they have been sketchy, and you know it. If you wish, merely say, "No thank you, I have nothing further to add." This is a point where you can "talk yourself out" of a good impression or fail to present an important bit of information. Remember, *you close the interview yourself*.

The chairman will then say, "That is all, Mr. _____, thank you." Do not be startled; the interview is over, and quicker than you think. Thank him, gather your belongings and take your leave. Save your sigh of relief for the other side of the door.

How to put your best foot forward

Throughout this entire process, you may feel that the board individually and collectively is trying to pierce your defenses, seek out your hidden weaknesses and embarrass and confuse you. Actually, this is not true. They are obliged to make an appraisal of your qualifications for the job you are seeking, and they want to see you in your best light. Remember, they must interview all candidates and a non-cooperative candidate may become a failure in spite of their best efforts to bring out his qualifications. Here are 15 suggestions that will help you:

1) Be natural – Keep your attitude confident, not cocky

If you are not confident that you can do the job, do not expect the board to be. Do not apologize for your weaknesses, try to bring out your strong points. The board is interested in a positive, not negative, presentation. Cockiness will antagonize any board member and make him wonder if you are covering up a weakness by a false show of strength.

2) Get comfortable, but don't lounge or sprawl

Sit erectly but not stiffly. A careless posture may lead the board to conclude that you are careless in other things, or at least that you are not impressed by the importance of the occasion. Either conclusion is natural, even if incorrect. Do not fuss with your clothing, a pencil or an ashtray. Your hands may occasionally be useful to emphasize a point; do not let them become a point of distraction.

3) Do not wisecrack or make small talk

This is a serious situation, and your attitude should show that you consider it as such. Further, the time of the board is limited – they do not want to waste it, and neither should you.

4) Do not exaggerate your experience or abilities

In the first place, from information in the application or other interviews and sources, the board may know more about you than you think. Secondly, you probably will not get away with it. An experienced board is rather adept at spotting such a situation, so do not take the chance.

5) If you know a board member, do not make a point of it, yet do not hide it

Certainly you are not fooling him, and probably not the other members of the board. Do not try to take advantage of your acquaintanceship – it will probably do you little good.

6) Do not dominate the interview

Let the board do that. They will give you the clues – do not assume that you have to do all the talking. Realize that the board has a number of questions to ask you, and do not try to take up all the interview time by showing off your extensive knowledge of the answer to the first one.

7) Be attentive

You only have 20 minutes or so, and you should keep your attention at its sharpest throughout. When a member is addressing a problem or question to you, give him your undivided attention. Address your reply principally to him, but do not exclude the other board members.

8) Do not interrupt

A board member may be stating a problem for you to analyze. He will ask you a question when the time comes. Let him state the problem, and wait for the question.

9) Make sure you understand the question

Do not try to answer until you are sure what the question is. If it is not clear, restate it in your own words or ask the board member to clarify it for you. However, do not haggle about minor elements.

10) Reply promptly but not hastily

A common entry on oral board rating sheets is "candidate responded readily," or "candidate hesitated in replies." Respond as promptly and quickly as you can, but do not jump to a hasty, ill-considered answer.

11) Do not be peremptory in your answers

A brief answer is proper – but do not fire your answer back. That is a losing game from your point of view. The board member can probably ask questions much faster than you can answer them.

12) Do not try to create the answer you think the board member wants

He is interested in what kind of mind you have and how it works – not in playing games. Furthermore, he can usually spot this practice and will actually grade you down on it.

13) Do not switch sides in your reply merely to agree with a board member

Frequently, a member will take a contrary position merely to draw you out and to see if you are willing and able to defend your point of view. Do not start a debate, yet do not surrender a good position. If a position is worth taking, it is worth defending.

14) Do not be afraid to admit an error in judgment if you are shown to be wrong

The board knows that you are forced to reply without any opportunity for careful consideration. Your answer may be demonstrably wrong. If so, admit it and get on with the interview.

15) Do not dwell at length on your present job

The opening question may relate to your present assignment. Answer the question but do not go into an extended discussion. You are being examined for a *new* job, not your present one. As a matter of fact, try to phrase ALL your answers in terms of the job for which you are being examined.

Basis of Rating

Probably you will forget most of these "do's" and "don'ts" when you walk into the oral interview room. Even remembering them all will not ensure you a passing grade. Perhaps you did not have the qualifications in the first place. But remembering them will help you to put your best foot forward, without treading on the toes of the board members.

Rumor and popular opinion to the contrary notwithstanding, an oral board wants you to make the best appearance possible. They know you are under pressure – but they also want to see how you respond to it as a guide to what your reaction would be under the pressures of the job you seek. They will be influenced by the degree of poise you display, the personal traits you show and the manner in which you respond.

ABOUT THIS BOOK

This book contains tests divided into Examination Sections. Go through each test, answering every question in the margin. We have also attached a sample answer sheet at the back of the book that can be removed and used. At the end of each test look at the answer key and check your answers. On the ones you got wrong, look at the right answer choice and learn. Do not fill in the answers first. Do not memorize the questions and answers, but understand the answer and principles involved. On your test, the questions will likely be different from the samples. Questions are changed and new ones added. If you understand these past questions you should have success with any changes that arise. Tests may consist of several types of questions. We have additional books on each subject should more study be advisable or necessary for you. Finally, the more you study, the better prepared you will be. This book is intended to be the last thing you study before you walk into the examination room. Prior study of relevant texts is also recommended. NLC publishes some of these in our Fundamental Series. Knowledge and good sense are important factors in passing your exam. Good luck also helps. So now study this Passbook, absorb the material contained within and take that knowledge into the examination. Then do your best to pass that exam.

EXAMINATION SECTION

EXAMINATION SECTION
TEST 1

DIRECTIONS: Each question or incomplete statement is followed by several suggested answers or completions. Select the one that BEST answers the question or completes the statement. *PRINT THE LETTER OF THE CORRECT ANSWER IN THE SPACE AT THE RIGHT.*

1. Of the following, the MOST valuable and desirable trait in a supervisor is a(n)

    A. ability to get the best work out of his men
    B. ability to inspire his men with the desire to *get ahead in the world*
    C. persuasive manner of speech
    D. tall and commanding appearance

1.____

2. The park supervisor who is MOST suitable for the general practical needs of the park department is the one who

    A. gets a great deal of satisfactory work done although usually handicapped by constant bickering among his subordinates
    B. gets a great deal of satisfactory work done because of his ability to do a large amount of it himself
    C. gets less work done than the other supervisors but has unusually high quality work production standards
    D. gets more than an average amount of satisfactory work done because of the cooperative way in which the men work for him

2.____

3. A park supervisor has been transferred to a new section. The BEST way for him to get cooperation from his subordinates would be to

    A. ask the superintendent to give him strong support
    B. explain his policy firmly so that the men cannot blame him for any mistakes made
    C. note the troublemakers and have them transferred out
    D. show his men that he not only is interested in getting work done but also has their welfare in mind

3.____

4. A knowledge of the experience and abilities of the subordinates working under him is MOST useful to a supervisor in

    A. deciding what type of discipline to exercise when necessary
    B. finding the cause of minor accidents on the job
    C. making proper work assignments
    D. making vacation schedules

4.____

5. A supervisor will be able to train his subordinates better if he is familiar with basic principles of learning. Which one of the following statements about the learning process is MOST correct?

    A. A subordinate who learns one job quickly will learn any other job quickly.
    B. Emphasizing correct things done by the subordinate usually gives him an incentive to improve.
    C. Great importance placed on a subordinate's mistakes is the best way to help him to get rid of them.
    D. It is very hard to teach new methods to middle-aged or older subordinates.

5.____

6. Several experienced employees have resigned. You have decided to arrange for permanent transfers of other experienced employees in your section to fill their jobs, leaving only jobs that new, inexperienced employees can fill easily. For you, the park supervisor, to talk this over with the employees who will be affected by the move would be

   A. *bad;* it would show weakness and wavering by you
   B. *bad;* transfers should be made on the basis of efficiency
   C. *good;* it will help you get better cooperation from the employees involved
   D. *good;* transfer should be made on the basis of seniority

6.____

7. An assistant gardener under your supervision does much less work than he is capable of. What should be your FIRST step in an effort to improve his performance?

   A. Discovering why he is not working up to his full capacity
   B. Going over his mistakes and shortcomings with him to reduce them
   C. Pointing out to him that the quality of his work is below standard
   D. Showing him that the other men produce much more than he does

7.____

8. The first thing a certain park supervisor does when he assigns a subordinate to a new job is to find out what the man already knows about the job. This practice is

   A. *good;* mainly because the subordinate may know more than the supervisor about the job
   B. *good;* mainly because this information will help the supervisor in instructing the subordinate
   C. *poor;* mainly because since it's a new job the subordinate can't be expected to know anything
   D. *poor;* mainly because the supervisor should first find out how the subordinate will feel toward the job

8.____

9. Jones and Smith, who work together, do slightly more than an average amount of work for two men together. But you find that Jones does most of the work while Smith does less than he should. To correct this situation, the BEST thing for you as supervisor to do would be to

   A. assign work to Smith for which he must be personally responsible
   B. make a complaint to the superintendent about Smith, but praise Jones
   C. point out to Jones that he does most of the work and that he should urge Smith to do more
   D. require Smith to do more whenever the work of both men altogether falls below the expected average

9.____

10. You have given a new subordinate detailed instructions on how he should do a job. When you return a little later you find that the subordinate was afraid to start the job because he did not completely understand your instructions. In this situation, it would be BEST for you to

    A. assign the subordinate to a job where less intelligence is needed
    B. explain again, illustrating if possible how the job is to be done
    C. explain again, and recommend him for dropping at the end of probation if he does not understand
    D. make the subordinate explain why he did not at least start the job

10.____

11. A gardener does very good work but he has trouble getting to work on time. To get the man to come on time, the supervisor should

    A. bring him up on charges to stop the lateness once and for all
    B. have him report to the superintendent every time he is late
    C. talk over the problem with him to find its cause and possible solution
    D. threaten to transfer him if he cannot get to work early

12. As supervisor, you observe that an assistant gardener keeps making mistakes. Of the following, the BEST thing for you to do would be to

    A. make no mention of these mistakes as they gradually disappear with experience
    B. point the mistakes out to this man in front of the other subordinates so all may learn from them
    C. talk to the man privately about these mistakes and show him how to avoid them
    D. try to transfer this man out in exchange for a subordinate who can do the work

13. Proper action by the supervisor could MOST probably prevent work delays in his section caused by

    A. a large number of subordinates quitting their jobs in the park department
    B. the daily assignments of the subordinates not being properly planned
    C. the inexperience of new subordinates transferred into his section
    D. unexpected delays in delivery of material

14. If, after careful thought, you have definitely decided that one of your subordinates should be disciplined, it is MOST important for you to realize that

    A. discipline is the best tool for leading subordinates
    B. discipline should be severe in order to get the best results
    C. the discipline should be delayed so that its full force can be felt
    D. the subordinate should know why he is being disciplined

15. Your superior has sent to you for planting in your section a type of shrubbery which, in your opinion, is not suitable for the area. In this situation, it would be BEST for you to

    A. plant the shrubbery since your superior is responsible
    B. send the shrubbery back and ask for material suitable for the area
    C. talk it over with the subordinates under you to see if they think as you do
    D. talk the matter over with your superior right away

16. In repairing a crack in concrete, it is important to

    A. keep the patch dry until it hardens
    B. level the patch with the old surface while the concrete is quite wet
    C. smooth the edges of the crack before filling
    D. wet the old concrete surface when applying a patch

17. A usual method of *curing* concrete is to

    A. add common salt
    B. expose it to the sun
    C. keep it damp
    D. mix it for the proper period of time

18. Which one of the following statements about the operation of the steam heating system of a building is NOT correct?

    A. A disadvantage of draining the boiler each heating season is that air is admitted when the boiler is refilled.
    B. Hammering in the steam pipes indicates interference with the circulation of the water.
    C. Proper operation of radiator air-vent valves is indicated when steam escapes continuously from the valves.
    D. Rising level of water in the boiler may indicate a worn washer in the valve admitting water to the boiler

19. A smoking chimney connected to an oil burner system may indicate a(n)

    A. clogged chimney   B. oversupply of air
    C. undersupply of air   D. undersupply of oil

20. As compared to brass pipe, copper tubing has the advantage of

    A. being a lot cheaper
    B. being more flexible
    C. having a smooth surface
    D. requiring no special fittings

21. An air cushion in a water plumbing system will

    A. confine sewer gas
    B. increase water pressure
    C. prevent chattering when the faucet is partly open
    D. prevent water hammer

22. A short piece of pipe threaded on the outside at both ends is usually called a

    A. coupling   B. nipple   C. joint   D. union

23. The MOST important purpose of a trap placed in a wasteline beneath a sink is to

    A. block sewer gas   B. catch dirt
    C. provide a cleanout   D. provide venting

24. The one of the following which has the same purpose as a fuse in an electrical system is a

    A. circuit breaker   B. condenser
    C. relay   D. transformer

25. New galvanized iron fixtures are BEST prepared for painting by

    A. cleaning with steel wool
    B. finishing with emery cloth
    C. scouring with cleanser powder
    D. washing with vinegar solution

KEY (CORRECT ANSWERS)

1. A
2. D
3. D
4. C
5. B
6. C
7. A
8. B
9. A
10. B
11. C
12. C
13. B
14. D
15. D
16. D
17. C
18. C
19. C
20. B
21. D
22. B
23. A
24. A
25. D

TEST 2

DIRECTIONS: Each question or incomplete statement is followed by several suggested answers or completions. Select the one that BEST answers the question or completes the statement. *PRINT THE LETTER OF THE CORRECT ANSWER IN THE SPACE AT THE RIGHT.*

1. Blistering of paint on an outside wall is MOST likely to be caused by too

    A. little sunlight hitting the wall
    B. much moisture from inside the building
    C. much moisture from outside the building
    D. much sunlight hitting the wall

    1.____

2. Which of the following is MOST likely to be caused by putting a hard finish coat of paint over a soft primer?

    A. Alligatoring B. Chalking
    C. Flaking   D. Wrinkling

    2.____

3. For cleaning shellac from a brush, it is BEST to use

    A. benzine   B. denatured alcohol
    C. lacquer thinner D. turpentine

    3.____

4. Emery cloth is usually used as a(n)

    A. mulch   B. abrasive
    C. pipe covering D. waterproof covering

    4.____

5. To remove dirt spots from asphalt floor tile, it is BEST to use

    A. benzine   B. carbon tetrachloride
    C. soap and water D. turpentine

    5.____

6. A carbide tipped drill is ordinarily required for drilling in

    A. aluminum   B. cast iron
    C. hard steel D. masonry

    6.____

7. A toggle bolt is usually MOST suitable for attaching objects to

    A. hollow masonry   B. thick brick walls
    C. thick concrete walls D. studs or beams

    7.____

8. Authorities on park maintenance often recommend that large picnic tables be anchored to the ground. The MAIN reason given is that such anchoring

    A. keeps the picnic tables in even rows
    B. prevents damage caused by moving
    C. prevents theft by the public
    D. restricts picnicking to picnic grounds

    8.____

9. Calcium chloride is useful on a tennis court for

    A. keeping dust down   B. keeping the surface packed down
    C. marking the court   D. reflecting the heat

    9.____

10. The MAIN reason a fireplace built with a chimney is NOT recommended for picnic areas at beaches and parks is that such fireplaces   10._____

    A. are hard to maintain
    B. cost so much to construct
    C. increase the danger of fire
    D. provide too much draft

11. The type of outdoor fireplace which is MOST economical and easiest to maintain is   11._____

    A. an entirely concrete fireplace
    B. an upright steel charcoal burner
    C. one made of cement mixed with asbestos
    D. one made of masonry lined with firebrick

12. Copper sulphate is MOST likely to be used in the operation of a swimming pool   12._____

    A. as a paint
    B. as a water softener
    C. for control of algae
    D. for filtering the water

13. The inspection of a wading pool to determine if it is in good condition does NOT usually include a check of   13._____

    A. expansion joints for tightness
    B. foots at base of fence for lead
    C. porous blocks for drainage
    D. valve pit for debris

14. A program of preventive maintenance for equipment which includes periodic inspection and upkeep is MOST likely to result in   14._____

    A. fewer large scale repairs because repairs can be made before they become more serious
    B. higher labor costs for repairs since single repairs rather than an accumulation of repairs are made at one time
    C. less total productive time from each piece of equipment because of the periodic removal from service
    D. the need for more standby equipment to replace equipment taken out of service

15. The one of the following which will probably contribute MOST to keeping park areas in a clean and orderly condition is a   15._____

    A. large number of receptacles for refuse
    B. large number of signs strategically placed
    C. distribution of park department rules and regulations to park users
    D. spirit of cooperation on the part of the public

16. The addition of organic matter to the soil is   16._____

    A. good for both clay soils and for sandy soils
    B. good for clay soils but not for sandy soils
    C. good for sandy soils but not for clay soils
    D. not recommended for dry soils

17. Animal manure should usually be added to the soil when the manure is   17.____

    A. completely dried out
    B. not yet rotted
    C. partially rotted
    D. sure to come in contact with plant roots

18. Which one of these materials is organic?   18.____

    A. Lime   B. Muriate of potash
    C. Peat   D. Superphosphate

19. The three plant food elements which are usually NOT present in the soil in sufficient   19.____
    amounts needed by plants are

    A. nitrogen, calcium, sulphur
    B. nitrogen, phosphorus, potassium
    C. phosphorus, hydrogen, carbon
    D. potassium, magnesium, sulphur

20. A change in the pH of a soil from 6.5 to 7.5 indicates that the soil   20.____

    A. has a greater moisture content
    B. has become neutral
    C. is more acid
    D. is more alkaline

21. An acid soil is indicated if upon contact with the soil _____ litmus paper turns _____.   21.____

    A. blue; purple   B. blue; red
    C. red; blue   D. red; purple

22. Of the following, the MOST correct statement about fertilizers is that   22.____

    A. a fertilizer may consist of a single plant food element or of a combination of several
       plant food elements
    B. an inorganic fertilizer is made up of natural plant foods such as decomposed vege-
       table and animal substances
    C. an organic fertilizer is one produced commercially out of a combination of various
       chemicals
    D. the purpose of fertilizers is to kill insect pests as well as to feed plants

23. A bag of 10-6-4 fertilizer contains   23.____

    A. 10 percent nitrogen   B. 4 percent phosphorus
    C. 10 percent potash   D. 6 percent nitrogen

24. Which of these is a temporary grass?   24.____

    A. Creeping bent   B. Creeping red fescue
    C. Kentucky bluegrass   D. Redtop

25. An established lawn should usually be rolled one or two times, _____, in the _____.   25.____

    A. heavily; fall   B. heavily; summer
    C. lightly; fall   D. lightly; spring

KEY (CORRECT ANSWERS)

1. C
2. A
3. B
4. B
5. C

6. D
7. A
8. B
9. A
10. D

11. B
12. C
13. C
14. A
15. D

16. A
17. C
18. C
19. B
20. D

21. B
22. A
23. A
24. D
25. D

TEST 3

DIRECTIONS: Each question or incomplete statement is followed by several suggested answers or completions. Select the one that BEST answers the question or completes the statement. *PRINT THE LETTER OF THE CORRECT ANSWER IN THE SPACE AT THE RIGHT.*

1. As compared with other grasses, common Bermuda grass has the DISADVANTAGE that it   1.____

    A. can easily crowd out other desirable plants
    B. cannot stand intense summer heat
    C. cannot stand much wear
    D. is particularly subject to pests and diseases

2. After a new lawn is seeded, it should be   2.____

    A. covered with at least 1/4 inch of soil
    B. kept moist until the grass is well up
    C. raked lightly for several days
    D. watered with a heavy spray

3. Frequent light watering of lawns is MOST likely to   3.____

    A. cause erosion
    B. prevent fungus diseases
    C. result in a dense luxuriant turf
    D. result in shallow root systems

4. The one of the following which is suitable for use against crab grass in a lawn is   4.____

    A. DDT   B. lindane
    C. potassium cyanate   D. 2, 4-D

5. In the maintenance of an established lawn, it is NOT considered good practice to   5.____

    A. fertilize in hot and dry summer weather
    B. leave lawn clippings on the ground
    C. remove fallen leaves from the lawn
    D. water thoroughly during dry spells

6. Plugs are   6.____

    A. a type of grass seed
    B. grass roots cut into bits
    C. small circular cuts of sod
    D. small sprigs of grass

7. The MAIN chemical ingredients in bordeaux mixture are   7.____

    A. copper sulphate and lime
    B. copper sulphate and sulphur
    C. nicotine sulphate and copper
    D. sulphur and lime

8. Privet planted as hedge material should usually be set about _____ inches apart.

    A. 3   B. 9   C. 18   D. 24

9. A hedge should be cut so that it is narrower at the top than at the bottom. This practice is

    A. *bad;* it does not let sunlight get to the base of the hedge
    B. *bad;* it stunts the growth of the hedge
    C. *good;* it is done to allow sunlight to get to the lower leaves
    D. *good;* it is done to speed up growth

10. The transplanting of deciduous trees in full leaf is not recommended, but it may be done successfully if the whole plant is sprayed with special plastic to cover both sides of the leaves. The MOST important reason for the success of such a practice is that it helps

    A. preserve the bark
    B. preserve the leaves
    C. prevent sun scald
    D. prevent water loss

11. If a tree is to be transplanted from its natural habitat, it is desirable to root prune it at least one growing season in advance MAINLY in order to

    A. increase its resistance to disease
    B. induce growth of new roots in a fibrous mass
    C. reduce its requirements for moisture and nutrients
    D. reduce top growth

12. The top of a deciduous tree is often cut back severely when the tree is transplanted bare rooted. The MAIN purpose of this cutting back is to

    A. allow sun to get at the bark
    B. help the tree withstand the wind
    C. make it easier to move the tree
    D. make up for root loss

13. Of the following trees, the one which grows BEST in the east coast is the

    A. ginkgo   B. larch   C. sour gum   D. sweet gum

14. Which of these is an evergreen?

    A. American elm
    B. Honey locust
    C. Norway maple
    D. Weeping hemlock

15. It is recommended that a shrub which bears blossoms on last year's wood be pruned soon after it has bloomed. This recommendation is

    A. *bad,* because pruning should not be done during a period of very active growth
    B. *bad,* because such pruning should not be done when the plant is in a weakened condition
    C. *good,* because such pruning helps the plant put its energy into desirable growth
    D. *good,* because then the pruning is done when the plant is least exposed to disease

Questions 16-19.

DIRECTIONS: Questions 16 through 19 are to be answered on the basis of the paragraph given below. Your answers to these questions must be based only on the information given in this paragraph.

Maintenance of leased or licensed areas on public parks or lands has always been a problem. A good rule to follow in the administration and maintenance of such areas is to limit the responsibility of any lessee or licensee to the maintenance of the structures and grounds essential to the efficient operation of the concession, not including areas for the general use of the public, such as picnic areas, public comfort stations, etc., except where such facilities are leased to another public agency or where special conditions make such inclusion practicable, and where a good standard of maintenance can be assured and enforced. If local conditions and requirements are such that public use areas are included, adequate safeguards to the public should be written into contracts and enforced in their administration, to insure that maintenance by the concessionaire shall be equal to the maintenance standards for other park property.

16. According to the above paragraph, when an area on a public park is leased to a concessionaire, it is usually BEST to

   A. confine the responsibility of the concessionaire to operation of the facilities and leave the maintenance function to the park agency
   B. exclude areas of general public use from the maintenance obligation of the concessionaire
   C. make the concessionaire responsible for maintenance of the entire area, including areas of general public use
   D. provide additional comfort station facilities for the area

17. According to the above paragraph, a valid reason for giving a concessionaire responsibility for maintenance of a picnic area within his leased area is that

   A. local conditions and requirements made it practicable
   B. more than half of the picnic area falls within his leased area
   C. the concessionaire has leased picnic facilities to another public agency
   D. the picnic area falls entirely within his leased area

18. According to the above paragraph, a precaution that should be taken when a concessionaire is made responsible for maintenance of an area of general public use in a park is

   A. making sure that another public agency has not previously been made responsible for this area
   B. providing the concessionaire with up-to-date equipment, if practicable
   C. requiring that the concessionaire take out adequate insurance for the protection of the public
   D. writing safeguards to the public into the contract

19. According to the above paragraph, the level of maintenance performed by a concessionaire on an area of general public use for which he is responsible should be

   A. equal to standards for other park property only if special conditions make this practicable
   B. equivalent to that on any other public property
   C. equivalent to that on other areas of the park
   D. higher than in other surrounding areas

Questions 20-23.

DIRECTIONS: Questions 20 through 23 refer to the sprayer described in the following paragraph.

This is a hydraulic, power wheelbarrow sprayer with a tank capacity of 20 gallons. It is equipped with piston type pumps which deliver at maximum 1.5 gpm. Power is furnished by a small air-cooled engine.

20. The sprayer described in the above paragraph is MOST likely to be used for

   A. sanitation spraying
   B. spraying small lawns and shrubs
   C. spraying tall shade trees
   D. treating large areas for mosquito control

21. The word *hydraulic* used to describe this sprayer indicates MOST probably that

   A. compressed air carries the particles of spray
   B. liquid pressure plays an important part in the operation of the sprayer
   C. oil is an important part of the mixture sprayed
   D. the mixture which is sprayed has a high percentage of water

22. The piston in the pump described in the above paragraph is probably MOST NEARLY like a

   A. gear   B. hollow open tube
   C. solid cylinder   D. wheel

23. If the sprayer described above used up the complete contents of a full tank in 16 minutes, it would be delivering at less than its maximum rate by _____ gallon per minute.

   A. 3/4   B. 1/2   C. 1/6   D. 1/4

24. The MAIN reason why a park supervisor should be familiar with the principles and practices of report writing is that he

   A. can then understand the reports issued by the Department better
   B. might be promoted to an administrative position
   C. must be able to write a report if an emergency should occur
   D. must submit reports in connection with his work

25. Of the following, the BEST reason why a park supervisor should prepare a report on an unusual incident as soon as possible after it happens is that
 A. he might forget some of the facts if he waits
 B. he might not have time to do so later on
 C. this gives his supervisor the opportunity to review his report before anyone else sees it
 D. this proves that he was on the job

KEY (CORRECT ANSWERS)

1.	A	11.	B
2.	B	12.	D
3.	D	13.	A
4.	C	14.	D
5.	A	15.	C
6.	C	16.	B
7.	B	17.	A
8.	B	18.	D
9.	C	19.	C
10.	D	20.	B

21.	B
22.	C
23.	D
24.	D
25.	A

TEST 4

DIRECTIONS: Each question or incomplete statement is followed by several suggested answers or completions. Select the one that BEST answers the question or completes the statement. *PRINT THE LETTER OF THE CORRECT ANSWER IN THE SPACE AT THE RIGHT.*

1. The FIRST step usually taken in writing a report is to   1.____

    A. decide how long the report should be
    B. determine how many copies of the report will be needed
    C. determine what is to be included in the report
    D. read copies of other reports of a similar nature

2. The introduction or beginning of a report on a certain procedure in an organization usually should NOT contain   2.____

    A. a brief statement of the conclusions reached
    B. a statement of the subject of the report
    C. examples of procedures in other organizations
    D. the reason for the report

3. An example of a periodic report is a(n)   3.____

    A. monthly activities report
    B. accident report
    C. probationary report on an employee
    D. report on the effectiveness of a new procedure

4. The one of the following which is NOT an important reason for requiring a complete report of an accident is that   4.____

    A. employees should receive proper training in the writing of complete reports
    B. it is desirable to have a full record of all accidents
    C. the report can be used as a basis for determining the cause of the accident
    D. the report can be used as a basis for eliminating the cause of such accidents in the future

5. A vandalism report on damage to a certain comfort station states: *The copper metal lining the intersection of chimney with roof was completely cut away.* Too many words are used in this report to describe the   5.____

    A. eaves trough   B. flashing
    C. wainscoting   D. weather stripping

6. Which of the following is prohibited in a park, without exception, by the rules and regulations of the department of parks?   6.____

    A. Capturing a pigeon
    B. Feeding popcorn to squirrels
    C. Kindling a wood fire
    D. Remaining after 12:00 midnight

7. According to the rules and regulations of the department of parks, a licensed ambulance on emergency service using a parkway under the jurisdiction of the department is

   A. not permitted to sound its siren unless there is a traffic jam
   B. permitted to exceed the maximum speed limit prescribed for other vehicles
   C. subject to all traffic regulations for other vehicles
   D. to be given the right of way by other vehicles

8. According to the rules and regulations of the department of parks, a motorist who gets a flat tire on an improved or paved park roadway must

   A. continue slowly to a point beyond the nearest park exit where he may then change the tire
   B. get the vehicle completely off the roadway in order to remove and replace the tire
   C. have the vehicle towed to the nearest exit by a tow truck which has a permit issued by the Commissioner of Parks
   D. put a person or warning device seventy feet to the rear of the vehicle while making repairs on the roadway

9. With respect to permits issued to carry on any activity in a park, it is MOST correct to state that

   A. permits are not required for organized picnics or outings
   B. permits for the use of parks in which there is located a botanical or zoological society require the approval of the society
   C. the permit will not be issued if it is desired for the purpose of conducting an affair of a private or commercial nature
   D. when the permit is revoked, the fee must be refunded

10. The preferred minimum distance from the ground for the lowest limb of a tree in a park playground is _____ feet.

    A. 5   B. 6   C. 7   D. 8

11. The permit for digging a hole to plant a street tree in a borough is issued by the

    A. Director
    B. Office of the County Executive
    C. Department of Highways
    D. Senior Horticulturist of the Department of Parks

12. In playgrounds operated jointly by the department of parks and the board of education, the board of education is USUALLY responsible for

    A. their maintenance
    B. their operation during school hours, except for areas set aside for mothers and pre-school age children
    C. their operation during the summer and weekends, except for areas set aside for mothers and pre-school age children
    D. the supervision of the kindergarten section at all times

13. If a new maintenance procedure has been adopted, the supervisor should keep this work under his close super vision until the procedure has become routine. Of the following, the MOST important reason for doing this is to

    A. impress the workers with the importance of the job
    B. get the work done as quickly as possible
    C. make certain that the workers are following the procedure correctly
    D. find out how long the job should take

14. Assume that a supervisor is preparing a report recommending that a standard work procedure be changed.
    Of the following, the MOST important information that he should include in this report is

    A. the type and amount of re-training that will be needed
    B. a complete description of the present procedure
    C. the opinion of his supervisor
    D. the details and advantages of the recommended procedure

15. A supervisor tells a maintainer to make certain changes on a job which the maintainer has just completed. The maintainer tells the supervisor that he feels the changes are not necessary.
    The supervisor should

    A. leave the job as it is and explain to his supervisor why the changes were not made
    B. save time by having another maintainer make the changes
    C. explain why the changes are to be made and insist this maintainer do it
    D. arrange a meeting for this maintainer with the supervisor's supervisor

16. When a ladder is used in working against the side of a building, for safest operation the base of the ladder should be placed at a distance from the building equal to APPROXIMATELY _____ the length of the ladder.

    A. 1/2   B. 1/3   C. 1/4   D. 1/5

17. Workers should not be allowed to work from ladders footed on open trucks. The MAIN reason for this is that the

    A. floor of a truck is not level
    B. floor of a truck is usually slippery
    C. truck might move unexpectedly
    D. truck might be scratched or otherwise damaged

18. The mist blower or concentrate sprayer is used MAINLY for

    A. application of liquid fertilizers
    B. control of grass, brush, or forest fires
    C. fly and mosquito control
    D. shade tree work

19. Of the following, the MOST satisfactory type of spade is one made with a

    A. heavy handle
    B. metal shank which extends part way up the handle

C. plastic handle
D. single sheet of metal pressed into shape

20. Portable generators are ideal for operating portable tools. The generator referred to in this statement is

   A. a type of battery
   B. a type of motor
   C. used for changing electrical energy into mechanical energy
   D. used for changing mechanical energy into electrical energy

21. Chains on a lawnmower work longer and better when they are

   A. lubricated once each year
   B. lubricated twice each year
   C. lubricated weekly and more frequently if necessary
   D. not lubricated

22. Of the following pieces of equipment, the one which is MOST efficient for mowing tall, coarse, tough grass is a large

   A. brush chipper
   B. reel mower
   C. rotary mower
   D. sickle bar mower

23. With spark plug out, hold thumb over spark plug hole while engine is rotated. When compression is felt, replace spark plug. This one step is recommended in preparation of a gasoline-driven lawnmower for winter storage. The MAIN reason such a step is taken is to

   A. avoid sticking of the valves later
   B. insure proper timing of valves later
   C. make sure valves are open
   D. put tension on the valves

24. A standard recommendation for operating a gasoline-driven mower is that the motor should warm up before the mower is put to use. The MAIN reason for this is to get the

   A. engine broken in before it carries any load
   B. proper clearance and lubrication for moving parts
   C. proper gas-air mixture at the carburetor
   D. proper timing for spark plug firing

25. Treat a running engine-driven rotary mower as you would a gun. This warning is MOST probably justified because

   A. objects flying from the mower blades can cause injury
   B. such mowers are, and should be, treated like precision instruments
   C. the mower should be treated with the care of a valued possession
   D. the mower should be well-oiled and housed

KEY (CORRECT ANSWERS)

1. C
2. C
3. A
4. A
5. B

6. A
7. C
8. B
9. C
10. D

11. B
12. B
13. C
14. D
15. C

16. C
17. C
18. D
19. B
20. D

21. D
22. C
23. A
24. B
25. A

EXAMINATION SECTION
TEST 1

DIRECTIONS: Each question or incomplete statement is followed by several suggested answers or completions. Select the one that BEST answers the question or completes the statement. *PRINT THE LETTER OF THE CORRECT ANSWER IN THE SPACE AT THE RIGHT.*

1. Which of the following is the BEST measure to take to discipline a worker for his first violation of a rule?

    A. Speak to him in private
    B. Point out his past mistakes
    C. Explain to him the grievance procedure
    D. Have some witnesses present

    1._____

2. When a supervisor gives verbal instructions to a maintainer about the procedure to follow in doing a certain job, the supervisor will MOST likely avoid confusing the maintainer if

    A. his instructions are clear and concise
    B. his instructions contain as many details as possible
    C. he gives the instructions to the maintainer as quickly as possible
    D. he repeats the instructions to the maintainer several times, each time using different words

    2._____

3. Of the following, the BEST procedure to follow if you see one of your men using the wrong tool in doing his work is to

    A. stop him from proceeding and let another maintainer finish this man's work
    B. stop him from proceeding and direct him to use the correct tool
    C. take the man aside after the job is finished and tell him not to use the wrong tool again
    D. reprimand him and avoid giving him this type of work in the future

    3._____

4. Of the following, the LEAST appropriate guide for a supervisor to follow in assigning his men to various jobs is for him to

    A. assign the work according to each man's ability
    B. allow his men to take on as many jobs as they think they can handle
    C. distribute the workload evenly
    D. combine similar jobs and assign them to the same men

    4._____

5. The term *shoestring parks* MOST correctly describes

    A. foot paths, bicycle paths, and passive recreational areas developed alongside the pavements of parkways
    B. recreational areas developed along the beach areas under the jurisdiction of the department of parks
    C. playgrounds and small parks developed on excess lands purchased for public housing projects
    D. play areas developed in conjunction with large public swimming pools

    5._____

6. A maintainer asks his supervisor a question about a new maintenance procedure with which the supervisor is not familiar.
Of the following actions, the BEST one for the supervisor to take is to tell the maintainer

   A. to try to logically figure out the new procedure
   B. to use the old method with which the maintainer is more familiar
   C. that he should try to find another supervisor who knows the answer
   D. that he will try to get the information for him

7. Of the following, the MOST important reason for having the employee suggestion program is that it

   A. makes employees realize that management's job is not an easy one
   B. is a suitable replacement for the *merit increase*
   C. saves the department money
   D. gives employees an alternate route for their grievance

8. The MOST important function of fences around playgrounds is that

   A. fences eliminate vandalism by keeping out the mischief makers and putting the playgrounds under complete control
   B. adequate fencing relieves the department of all liability in cases of injury occurring at times when the playground is locked
   C. children using a playground are less likely to be injured in auto accidents on streets adjacent to the playground if it is fenced
   D. fences add to the value of adjacent property by reducing trespassing by children using the playground

9. It has been suggested that where a playground borders on a busy street, the entrances should be at the corners rather than in the middle of the block. The MOST important basis for this suggestion is

   A. fencing costs will be reduced considerably by such construction
   B. children leaving the playground will not be able to run into the street between intersections
   C. clearing the playground of children will be accomplished more easily and in a more orderly fashion
   D. roads and paths will be reduced to the desired minimum

10. Chainlink fences are generally considered the MOST satisfactory fencing for playgrounds and athletic fields because

    A. their maintenance requirements are less than for iron picket fences
    B. they economize on space in playgrounds
    C. they enable the playground to be locked when not in use
    D. they fit into a landscaping design more satisfactorily than any other type of fence

11. The dimension of a standard city block is 800 feet by 200 feet. The acreage of this block is MOST NEARLY _____ acres.

    A. 4   B. 2 1/2   C. 8   D. 1 1/2

12. Of the following instructions concerning the reporting of an accident, the one which is LEAST correct is

    A. park conditions contributing to the cause of the accident should be noted
    B. note all damage to park property
    C. ascertain the name of the owner and license number if an auto was involved
    D. report on the condition of the brakes if an auto is involved

13. The park use for which a park permit is NOT required is

    A. an organized picnic or outing
    B. fishing in designated areas
    C. storage of boats on park lands
    D. private construction work not under contract with the commissioner

14. Assume that you are a supervisor and that a maintainer makes a complaint to you which has no merit.
    Of the following, the BEST way for you to handle this situation is to

    A. tell the maintainer not to bother you with worthless complaints
    B. keep the complaint on file and ignore it as long as possible
    C. forward the complaint to your assistant supervisor
    D. discuss the complaint with him and show him that his complaint is not justified

15. As a newly appointed supervisor, you find that one of your workers is a longtime friend whom you must now supervise.
    Of the following, your BEST course of action is to

    A. break off all relations with this employee
    B. attempt to separate your official actions from your personal attitudes
    C. do nothing unless the other men complain of favoritism on your part
    D. request that your friend be transferred to another supervisor

16. Of the following, the dual use of play space is MOST feasible in the case of a

    A. tennis court used for volleyball
    B. paddle tennis court used for regulation tennis
    C. golf course used for regulation baseball
    D. shuffleboard course used for paddle tennis

17. Of the following, a tree that is LEAST preferred for street planting is the

    A. pin oak   B. red maple
    C. plane   D. silver maple

18. The maintenance of newly planted street trees is the responsibility of the

    A. homeowner for the first year, and thereafter the department of parks
    B. department of parks as soon as the planting of the tree is completed
    C. both the home owner and the department of parks as soon as they are planted
    D. department of parks only if the home owner duly notifies the department that he wishes to relieve himself of responsibility

19. To maintain corn brooms and fibre brushes in good condition, the park supervisor should instruct his employees to

   A. avoid wetting them with water since they may become brittle if so treated
   B. treat the fibres with oil regularly to keep them flexible
   C. discard those brooms which have become worn down or are brittle
   D. wet them once or twice a week with warm water to prevent them from becoming brittle

20. During the summer season, the supervisor should maintain a cleaning schedule in which the floors of comfort station toilet rooms are swept

   A. and wet mopped daily
   B. and damp mopped daily and washed once a week
   C. daily and damp mopped weekly
   D. daily and mopped every other day

21. Of the following, the MOST important reason for NOT using deodorants in cleaning comfort station floors is deodorants

   A. may cover up the odor, but not eliminate the source
   B. have an unpleasant odor which requires excessive ventilation of the rooms
   C. may contain chemicals that will harm the surfaces cleaned
   D. reduce the effectiveness of cleaning solutions used on these floors

22. If the car which you are driving starts to skid on a wet pavement, the BEST way to overcome the skidding is to

   A. put on the emergency brake in addition to the foot brake
   B. release the brake and turn the steering wheel opposite to the direction in which the car is skidding
   C. release the brake and turn the steering wheel in the direction in which the car is skidding
   D. disengage the clutch and brake and try to keep the wheels straight ahead

23. Concerning the use of oil in crankcases of automobiles, it is CORRECT to say that

   A. lighter oils should be used in the wintertime
   B. lighter oils should be used in the summertime
   C. heavy oils should be used in the wintertime
   D. oil should not be changed if the oil gage shows full

24. The preferred method of eliminating growths of algae in a wading pool or swimming pool is to

   A. dose the water with copper sulphate
   B. increase the concentration of chlorine dosage
   C. empty the pool immediately upon discovering these growths
   D. spray the water surface with a 10% solution of D.D.T.

25. The routine of swimming pool operation includes

   A. tests of chlorine content of the water once a day
   B. cleaning filter beds with raw water rather than filtered water
   C. recirculation of water used in backwashing filter beds
   D. use of alum in the filter plants of the pool to form a floc

26. When the water in a wading pool appears excessively dirty, the MOST appropriate action the supervisor should take is to

   A. increase the rate of flow of water into the pool and clean the drains
   B. have the pool drained, cleaned, and refilled
   C. dose the pool more heavily with chlorine solution to reduce the possibility of infection spread
   D. forbid children to enter the pool unless they are clean

26.____

27. In preparing and maintaining a large wading pool for winter use as an ice skating rink, the supervisor should be careful to

   A. keep drainage outlets open to take up excess water
   B. build up the surface by applying water in thin film-like layers
   C. flood the area each morning to maintain the ice surface prepared previously
   D. apply water first to the area nearest the water sup-ply outlet and then proceed towards the far end

27.____

28. In maintaining clay tennis courts, the park foreman should have his employee apply calcium chloride to the surface primarily in order to

   A. reduce acidity of the surface
   B. keep dust down
   C. increase surface drainage
   D. keep the surface even

28.____

29. The material that is NOT used in marking the foul lines on a baseball field with a grass surface is

   A. white lead   B. lime
   C. cold water calcimine   D. whiting

29.____

30. Of the following, the statement that is CORRECT with respect to the maintenance of playground equipment is

   A. bearings of seesaws and swings should be greased daily to prevent excessive wear
   B. galvanized steel piping of jungle gyms should be oiled periodically during the summer to reduce rusting and deterioration
   C. bolts and nuts used on equipment should be checked daily for tightness and wear
   D. chutes of slides require daily waxing to preserve a smooth surface

30.____

31. The newer type of sandpits have irrigation systems for cleaning the sand. The advantage of these pits is that

   A. they require less maintenance than the older type
   B. they are less costly to install
   C. the sand surface need not be raked to remove debris
   D. the sand need not be replaced as frequently as in the older type

31.____

32. The manufacturer's name with which some lawnmowers in the department of parks are associated is

   A. Toro   B. Royer   C. Hardie   D. Kaiser

32.____

33. CORRECT practice with respect to the sprinkling of lawns includes the fact that

    A. regular sprinkling of lawns should begin in the early spring when the ground thaws
    B. sprinkling should always be continued on any one spot until the soil has become thoroughly drenched with water
    C. sprinkling should never be begun in the late afternoon or early evening
    D. whirling spray-type sprinklers should not be used unless the soil is excessively dry and powdery

34. Generally, it is better to seed a lawn in the fall than in the spring. Of the following, the BEST explanation for this gardening rule is

    A. the ground is dryer in the spring than in the fall
    B. tree shading is at a minimum in the fall
    C. pedestrian traffic over a lawn is at a minimum in the fall
    D. weed growth is less in the fall than in the spring

35. In mowing a lawn, the blades of the mower should usually be adjusted to maintain the height of the grass

    A. about one-half inch
    B. not less than one and one-half inches
    C. not less than three inches
    D. approximately one inch

36. In giving instructions to laborers assigned to mowing a lawn, it should be emphasized that

    A. mowing should be frequent in hot dry weather since grass grows rapidly during this period
    B. clippings should generally be removed after mowing when lawns are regularly mowed
    C. lawnmowers should be operated up to the trunks of surrounding trees to insure an even turf
    D. lawns should not be mowed when wet and soft to avoid injury to the turf

37. In the maintenance and operation of lawnmowers, the park groundskeeper should be sure that

    A. lawns are sprayed with water just before mowing
    B. the revolving blades are pressed close to the stationary or non-revolving blade, with no clearance, if possible
    C. lawns are raked clean before mowing is attempted
    D. lawns are raked clean after regular mowing

38. To overcome brown spots on a lawn, the groundskeeper should have the lawn treated with

    A. D.D.T.
    B. lead arsenate
    C. mercury compounds
    D. heavy water spray

39. 2,4-D is a chemical which the groundskeeper should use to

   A. control weed growth on lawns
   B. destroy Japanese beetle grubs in the soil
   C. control grass diseases
   D. destroy bark beetles

40. An ingredient that is NOT usually found in compost is

   A. lime
   B. calcium chloride
   C. manure
   D. leaves

KEY (CORRECT ANSWERS)

1. A	11. A	21. A	31. D
2. A	12. D	22. C	32. A
3. B	13. B	23. A	33. B
4. B	14. D	24. A	34. D
5. A	15. B	25. D	35. B
6. D	16. A	26. B	36. D
7. C	17. D	27. B	37. C
8. C	18. A	28. B	38. C
9. B	19. D	29. A	39. A
10. A	20. A	30. C	40. B

TEST 2

DIRECTIONS: Each question or incomplete statement is followed by several suggested answers or completions. Select the one that BEST answers the question or completes the statement. *PRINT THE LETTER OF THE CORRECT ANSWER IN THE SPACE AT THE RIGHT.*

1. In gathering leaves and twigs, the large wooden rake should be used with

   A. long sliding strokes, the prongs being lifted only to clear the debris
   B. short pull and push strokes to avoid tearing the sod
   C. brush strokes as with a broom
   D. long pushing strokes, forcing leaves and twigs away from you

2. The newer type of fountains installed in parks and playgrounds throws the water jet at an angle instead of vertically. It is thought that the newer type is superior because

   A. the desired height of the jet of water is obtained more easily
   B. such fountains are more attractive and fit in better with modern playground layouts
   C. the possibility of damage and vandalism is reduced
   D. the possibility of contamination of the water supply is reduced

3. Of the following, the MOST important reason for shutting off the water supply to drinking fountains in the late fall is

   A. there is less need for water in the late fall and winter
   B. to avoid vandalism due to reduction of forces after the summer season
   C. to avoid breakage of supply lines in the winter
   D. water supply lines to fountains are usually located below the frost line

4. Suppose that a laborer complains to you about flooding of low parts of walks and paths in his park after heavy rains.
   Of the following, the factor that you would NOT consider as a probable cause of flooding is the

   A. condition of catch basins in the park
   B. condition of the street sewer system adjacent to the park
   C. condition of drainage system of the comfort stations in the park
   D. clogging of drainage lines and inlets

5. The repainting of iron picket fences should preferably be scheduled for

   A. any time in the fall or early winter, depending only on the number of visitors to the park involved
   B. early mornings in the late summer or fall months because the temperature is low
   C. winter weather, since cold weather is an aid to quick drying of paint
   D. early afternoons of clear dry days in the late summer or early fall

6. A priming coat of red lead is usually painted on iron picket fences MAINLY because

   A. the color of the finish coat will show up better on red lead
   B. it cleans the metal surface of rust and other foreign particles
   C. it prevents rusting and corrosion of the iron fence
   D. it avoids blistering of the finish paint coat

7. A laborer has been assigned to a playground containing a comfort station which is heated by a low pressure oil burner in the wintertime. Your instructions to the laborer regarding the operation of the heating plant should include

   A. maintenance of steam pressure above 10 pounds
   B. daily cleaning of ignition electrodes
   C. daily replacement of boiler water to prevent rust formation
   D. inspection of water level daily before starting up

8. A wire brush is USUALLY used in

   A. removing rust stains from the porcelain surface of wash basins
   B. preparing iron surfaces for painting
   C. heavy sweeping of concrete and cement surfaces
   D. clearing roofs of comfort stations of accumulated rubbish

9. The tool which is LEAST likely to be used by a worker in the replacement and repair of wood slats of benches is

   A. hack saw   B. plane
   C. cross-cut saw   D. brace and bit

10. Seesaws should be inspected daily to

    A. determine the need for painting the wood parts
    B. check possible splintering of the seat ends
    C. avoid rusting of metal supports
    D. see that horizontal pipe supports are not more than 24 inches above the ground

11. For sharpening gardening and pruning shears, the tool used is a(n)

    A. whetstone   B. oil stone
    C. flat file   D. carborundum wheel

12. In a 1-2-4 concrete mix using 6 1/2 gallons of water per batch, the material that is used in the SMALLEST quantity is

    A. sand   B. cement   C. water   D. gravel

13. It is specified that a concrete pavement be laid over a base of 5" of cinders. The BEST reason for this is that the

    A. cinders act as a binder between the earth and the concrete
    B. cinders aid in carrying off sub-surface drainage
    C. cinders offer a firm base, thereby minimizing the possibility of hollows and ridges
    D. use of cinders reduces the amount of cement required

14. A supervisor should know what type of material has been covered in an employee training program. Of the following, the MOST important reason for this is that the supervisor

    A. can learn of any new developments or changes in work procedures
    B. can know more about his men's qualifications when making assignments
    C. can show his interest in the program and thus encourage his men to be more productive
    D. will know what training has not been covered and should be recommended for a future training program

15. As soon as plant materials arrive from a nursery, they should be heeled in. Doing this will 15.___

    A. prevent root growth until the plant is transplanted
    B. keep the soil in better condition
    C. prevent drying out of the roots
    D. make certain that leaves and branches are not crushed

16. If a foreman determines that he cannot meet the deadline on a certain written report that his supervisor has assigned to him, he should 16.___

    A. work to the deadline and then ask for an extension
    B. inform his supervisor of his difficulty before the deadline
    C. ask another foreman for assistance
    D. meet the deadline even if he has to submit an inadequate report

17. After a heavy snow and sleet storm, the FIRST job of a park foreman is to see that 17.___

    A. walks of his section are cleared and sanded
    B. any damage to trees and buildings in his section is noted
    C. he gets instructions from the general park foreman
    D. ice skating areas are cleared of loose snow and properly planed

18. In planning winter maintenance of parks, the task which merits LEAST attention is 18.___

    A. sanding and salting of icy walks
    B. removal of snow from newly-seeded lawn areas
    C. keeping catch basin inlets clear during winter thaws
    D. checking equipment and supplies required for winter maintenance

19. Suppose that a person appears at the tennis courts and asks for an appointment to play. He does not have his tennis permit with him. However, you recognize him since he played the previous day and did possess a permit then. Your action should be to 19.___

    A. accept him because he has paid the required fee and is, therefore, eligible to play
    B. deny him admittance because he probably has given his card to another person
    C. deny him admittance because only permit holders may play on courts requiring permits
    D. accept his request for an appointment if he promises to show his card to you within the week

20. To reduce possible vandalism in parks, the park supervisor should 20.___

    A. inform his employees to break up any groups of children who are not engaged in play activities
    B. have his employees search all youths who may possess knives or other tools used by vandals
    C. instruct his men to make frequent regular tours of their areas
    D. instruct his men to concentrate on vandalism prevention rather than the routine maintenance of their areas

21. Supervisors should instruct their subordinates in the proper procedure for the maintenance and display of the National flag from flagpoles. These instructions should provide that

    A. on Memorial Day the flag be flown at half mast until sunset
    B. the flag be hoisted slowly and not be allowed to touch the ground
    C. when renewing a halyard care should be taken that the old halyard is completely removed before the new one is strung through the pulley
    D. when the flag is to be flown at half mast it should be hoisted briskly to the peak before being lowered to half staff

22. Suppose that a woman complains to you that one of your men was abusive when told there was a flooded condition in a comfort station. Your FIRST action on this complaint should be to

    A. tell the general park foreman about the complaint and recommend punitive action
    B. inform the complainant that the employee would have his assignment changed
    C. inform the complainant that the employee would be spoken to and the flooded condition corrected
    D. tell the complainant that she was probably wrong since park employees are instructed to be courteous and cooperative

23. Suppose that a newly assigned temporary assistant gardener is found sleeping on a park bench after his scheduled lunch hour. He offers no excuse other than his sleepiness after lunch. The MOST appropriate action in this situation is to

    A. warn him not to repeat this apparent neglect of duties
    B. determine his efficiency by inspecting the area he was supposed to rake and clean
    C. send him home for the day after warning him that a temporary employee ought to watch his step
    D. question him further about his neglect of duties since he may not know how to perform his assignment

24. Suppose that you notice that there is chronic non-observance of a posted sign warning persons to stay off a lawn which has been recently reseeded. Your men are unable to enforce the notice by speaking to the violators. Your next step should be to

    A. issue an order that violators be forcibly removed from the lawn
    B. order the arrest of any violators who are adults and can understand the meaning of the sign
    C. prepare a report for your general park foreman recommending that all violators be summoned to court
    D. inform the general park foreman of the situation so that he can recommend appropriate police action

25. Suppose that you saw two men with revolvers robbing another person in a small park. The MOST advisable thing for you to do is

    A. apprehend the robbers and bring them to the nearest police station
    B. get in touch with the general park foreman to have him report the occurrence to the borough office for appropriate police action
    C. seek police assistance immediately
    D. call out to the robbers, warning them to desist from robbing persons in a public park

26. Suppose that you are instructing your men on safety pre-cautions to be observed by them. Of the following, a precaution that should be followed is

    A. lye may be used to clean paint brushes, but must be carefully handled so that the hands do not touch it
    B. in using a file, the user should wear gloves to protect his hand from the sharp end of the file
    C. when using steel wool, gloves should be worn or hands otherwise protected
    D. chisels before being used should be mushroomed

27. A person in a playground shows symptoms of sunstroke and suddenly loses consciousness. Of the following steps in the aid of this person, the one that is NOT correct is

    A. call a doctor immediately
    B. apply cold wet cloths to person's head
    C. give stimulants such as cold water, spirits of ammonia or coffee
    D. remove some of the person's clothing, if possible

28. A child slips on the entrance step of a comfort station and injures herself. The next day, a lawyer representing the child's family asks you for information concerning the accident. You should

    A. be cooperative, showing the lawyer a copy of the accident report and discussing the condition of the comfort station
    B. tell the lawyer that the consent of the parents will be necessary before he releases any information
    C. refuse to answer any questions asked by the lawyer concerning the park or accident
    D. refer the lawyer to the borough office for further information about the accident

29. To provide for at least the minimum of care in a playground where the assigned employee is ill for a day, the park foreman should

    A. ask his supervisor to request an additional employee from central headquarters to cover the playground during this period
    B. assign the least competent employee to cover this playground in addition to his regular assignment for disciplinary purposes
    C. have all his employees take turns in covering the playground during the day
    D. have his most reliable employee cover the playground for the day

30. When a park supervisor is assigned to a new section, it is his responsibility and duty to lay out and schedule the performance of the work in his section so that the proper standard of operation is obtained. In preparing the schedule of maintenance, the FIRST step the park supervisor should take is to

    A. observe the men at work in his section to determine personnel replacement needs
    B. determine the exact area of his section
    C. learn the number of employees assigned to the section
    D. determine the amount of work required in the parks and playgrounds of his section

31. Competent supervision of work includes the laying out of the sequence of operations to be performed by employees so that there is a minimum of lost time and the work is performed in an efficient manner. To carry out this phase of supervision, the park supervisor should

    A. refer to the superintendent all instances where laborers fail to follow out the specific instructions given by him
    B. discuss with his laborers the job he wants done before assigning them to do the job
    C. watch his laborers and other subordinates continuously to make certain that they work efficiently
    D. assign an efficient employee along with an inefficient employee to see that the required work is completed

32. A factor that merits LEAST consideration in the periodic ordering of maintenance supplies and equipment is

    A. number and types of playgrounds in the section
    B. number of employees assigned to the section
    C. condition and type of play area surfaces in the section
    D. extent to which play areas in the section have been used

33. An employee requests supplies which are not standard items. The park supervisor should handle this request by

    A. refusing to forward the requisition because the supplies are probably not needed
    B. refusing to order the supplies unless urgently needed
    C. having the employee explain his request to determine whether standard items might be ordered instead
    D. reviewing carefully the work habits of the employee since the request is unusual and does not follow standard procedure

34. To determine the efficiency of an employee assigned in charge of a playground, the MOST important guide is the

    A. amount of cleaning material used during the year
    B. attendance record during the year
    C. number of required repairs to playground surfaces and walks during the year
    D. appearance of the playground during the year

35. Two part-time rink attendants earn $6,240 and $6,220 per annum, respectively, exclusive of a bonus of $2,640 per annum. If both have a pension deduction of 20%, the difference in the pension deduction of the two attendants on a semi-monthly basis is

    A. $1.50   B. $.50   C. $1.00   D. $.25

36. Suppose you are asked to prepare service rating reports on your subordinates. A fact which would NOT be reported on the service rating form is

    A. length of time employee has worked in your section
    B. excessive lateness or absence
    C. length of time employee has been employed in the Department
    D. exact title of employee

37. With respect to a concession in his park, the park supervisor should see that the

    A. area within fifty feet of the concession is maintained in a clean condition by the concessionaire
    B. concession is not operated on Sundays unless specifically permitted by the general park foreman
    C. concession or a carretina is not located within fifty feet of a comfort station
    D. employees of the concessionaire are at least 18 years of age and are suffering from no communicable disease

38. Of the following, the statement that is MOST correct with respect to the maintenance of hedges is that

    A. hedges should be clipped in the winter or early spring before any growth begins
    B. hedges should not be trimmed at all until late summer after secondary growth occurs
    C. annual clipping of privet hedges should be done just after the first strong growth has slowed down
    D. flat tops are preferred to rounded tops because snow is shed more easily by flat tops

39. In general, parkway maintenance is LEAST dependent on the

    A. frequency of use of benches and paths
    B. types of trees planted along the parkway
    C. neighborhoods through which the parkway runs
    D. amount and kind of traffic

40. Of the following, the MOST important reason for the construction of marginal playgrounds in large parks is to

    A. reduce damage to lawns and landscaped areas by children
    B. permit installation of modern playground equipment in space specifically designed for its use
    C. increase the area available for open field sports
    D. reduce the cost of playground operation and maintenance

KEY (CORRECT ANSWERS)

1. A	11. B	21. D	31. B
2. D	12. C	22. C	32. B
3. C	13. B	23. A	33. C
4. C	14. B	24. D	34. D
5. D	15. C	25. C	35. D
6. C	16. B	26. C	36. C
7. D	17. A	27. C	37. A
8. B	18. B	28. D	38. C
9. A	19. C	29. D	39. B
10. B	20. C	30. D	40. A

EXAMINATION SECTION
TEST 1

DIRECTIONS: Each question or incomplete statement is followed by several suggested answers or completions. Select the one that BEST answers the question or completes the statement. *PRINT THE LETTER OF THE CORRECT ANSWER IN THE SPACE AT THE RIGHT.*

1. A type of depression or pit that may serve to drain, collect or store liquids is called a 1.____

   A. ditch B. gutter C. sump D. trench

2. The general name applied to the material that is spread on the ground around plants to prevent evaporation of water from the soil or the freezing of the roots is 2.____

   A. mulch B. mullock C. fertilizer D. mullion

3. The wire, rope, chain or rod that is attached to a tree, and which is used to steady the tree, is called a 3.____

   A. guy B. davit C. hoist D. bitt

4. A chemical used to kill weeds is called a 4.____

   A. pesticide B. herbicide C. fungicide D. arborcide

5. A mixture of cement or lime with sand and water which is used between bricks or stones in buildings is called 5.____

   A. epoxy B. putty C. concrete D. mortar

6. Coarse aggregate is the same as 6.____

   A. pumice B. cement
   C. crushed stone D. sand

7. The process of keeping the surface of concrete as wet as possible after the concrete is placed and hardened in order to prevent loss of water through evaporation is called 7.____

   A. floating B. damping C. curing D. checking

8. Plants that live for more than two years are called 8.____

   A. annuals B. perennials C. biennials D. semi-annuals

9. Which piece of equipment is run by compressed air? 9.____

   A. Drill press B. Impact wrench
   C. Soldering gun D. Jack hammer

QUESTIONS 10-13.

Answer questions 10-13 SOLELY on the basis of the information given in the paragraphs below.

NITROGEN AND PLANT GROWTH

Nitrogen is an essential element for plant growth. Its most important function is to stimulate vegatative development and it is, therefore, particularly necessary in the production of leaves and stems. If an excess of nitrogen is applied to the soil, it will result in an excessive growth of foliage at the expense of flowers and fruit. The cell walls of the stems will also become weakened and the plant's resistance to disease will be lowered.

Nitrogen is seldom found in the soil in a free state but is usually in combination with other elements. Soils are usually lowest in available nitrogen during the early spring months. It is at this season that quickly available nitrogenous fertilizers are of particular value.

10. According to the paragraph, an excess of nitrogen in plants is *likely to* produce

    A. strong healthy stems
    B. stronger resistance to disease
    C. too many leaves and stems
    D. too many flowers and fruit.

11. Weakened cell walls and decreased resistance to disease in plants are *likely to* occur because

    A. there is too much foliage on the plant
    B. there is not enough nitrogen in the soil
    C. there is too much nitrogen in the soil
    D. there are too many flowers or too much fruit on the plant

12. According to the above passage, one of the properties of nitrogen is that it

    A. seldom combines with other elements in the soil
    B. increase the production of flowers
    C. increases the growth of roots
    D. increases vegetative growth in a plant

13. In which months would soil *most likely* be LOWEST in nitrogen? Late

    A. March and early April
    B. June and early July
    C. September and early October
    D. December and early January

14. A person may appear to be accident-prone for a number of reasons. Which of the following would NOT usually be particularly associated with frequent accidents?

    A. Slow work habits
    B. Improper training
    C. Lack of physical coordination
    D. Working in cramped quarters

15. When removing a large branch from a tree, a pruner usually includes an undercut on the branch.
    The SPECIFIC purpose of the undercut is to

    A. stimulate the flow of sap to the area where the branch is taken off in order to stimulate growth of new branches
    B. prevent the branch that is being taken off from tearing off a strip of bark down the tree
    C. aid the wound from the cut off branch to heal quickly without decay or infection
    D. prevent an excessive growth of new branches from where the branch had been

16. A foreman sees one of his men start to cut a hedge so that it will be narrower at the bottom than at the top. The foreman stops the man and tells him to cut hedges in general so that they are narrower at the top than at the bottom. "Why?" asks the man.
    The foreman gave him the *generally accepted* reason, which is that

    A. rainfall will be able to run down the sides, and moisture will reach other parts of the hedge more quickly
    B. the broad base of the hedge will keep the hedge from being top-heavy and prevent it from toppling over during heavy winds
    C. sunlight will be able to reach all parts of the hedge, thereby helping to keep the growth of the entire hedge dense
    D. the hedge will be uniform from top to bottom since the top grows out much faster than the bottom

17. Concrete sidewalks are usually laid with a divider space every four or six feet rather than as one long ribbon.
    The reason for allowing the space is that in the summer the concrete in the sidewalk is *most likely* to

    A. contract   B. expand   C. sweat   D. soften

18. Some degree of shock accompanies all injuries. Symptoms of shock include all of the following EXCEPT

    A. a warm dry skin   B. a rapid, weak pulse
    C. enlarged pupils   D. irregular breathing

19. You are going to plant ivy in the circular flower bed pictured in Figure I. You have decided to plant them on the border of each of circles A, B, and C. The distance around each of the circles is as follows:
    A = 32 feet
    B = 20 feet
    C = 6 feet
    If you can plant 3 plants per foot, how many plants will you need?

    A. 100   B. 135   C. 156   D. 174

20. Nine out of ten people have never used a fire extinguisher. A trained person used a fire extinguisher 2 1/2 times more effectively than the average person does.
    These facts should motivate a foreman of a new crew exposed to possible fire hazards to

A. have a substitute for fire extinguishers on the job
B. rely only on experienced firemen for extinguishing fires
C. try to get men into his crew who are experienced in the use of fire extinguishers
D. give training to his men on the use of fire extinguishers

21. The crowbar, pick and shovel are three hand tools that can all be used *effectively* and *safely* in the process of

    A. splitting logs
    B. prying heavy objects
    C. making holes in stone
    D. digging up earth

22. Those tools which require the user to twist or turn one end in one direction while the other end is held fast in order to apply a force on an object are classified as torsion tools. Of the following, the one which would NOT be classified as a torsion tool is

    A. pliers
    B. wrench
    C. pinchbar
    D. screw driver

23. A portable heater used widely in severe weather to protect masonry, concrete and plaster from freezing and to provide warmth for workmen is the

    A. blowtorch
    B. salamander
    C. plumbers' furnace
    D. metal forge

24. In loading and unloading materials a variety of equipment is used.
    Of the following, the one which is generally NOT an accessory in moving materials onto and off trucks is a

    A. power shovel
    B. clam shell
    C. grease rack
    D. lift truck

25. Which one of the following pictures shows the top of a Phillips-type screw?

26. Which one of the following is called a box-end wrench?

27. A chisel is a hammer-struck tool. Some workmen grip the chisel with the fist to steady it and minimize the chances of glancing blows. The turn "glancing" refers here to the

    A. hammer striking the chisel off angle, thereby hitting the hand holding the chisel
    B. chisel bending or warping under the pressure of hammer blows
    C. hammer hitting with uneven force each time it contacts the chisel
    D. chisel striking the material to be cut straight on, instead of at an angle

28. Which one of the following BEST describes a *counters ink*? A

    A. tool designed to balance weight
    B. hammer used to shape sheet metal
    C. tool that enlarges the top part of a hole
    D. tool used to dig holes rapidly

29. Of the following, the MAIN reason that some electrical tools require the use of a 3-pronged plug is to

    A. prolong the life of the fuse
    B. avoid wasting electricity
    C. prolong the life of the cord
    D. properly ground them

30. Which of the following statements applies BEST to the care and use of a shovel?

    A. A shovel should not be waxed or greased immediately before using it.
    B. Dipping a shovel into a pail of water occasionally, while digging, makes the shovel easier to use.
    C. The leg muscles should not be permitted to take most of the load when shovelling.
    D. A shovel should lie flat on the ground when it is not being used.

31. Which is the SAFEST distance between the base of a 24-foot fully extended ladder and the base of the building against which it is placed?

    A. 3 feet   B. 6 feet   C. 9 feet   D. 12 feet

32. When instructing a man on how to lift a heavy object, you should advise him to

    A. stand as far from the load as possible
    B. keep the back as straight as possible
    C. lift by straightening his legs first and then his back
    D. lift from a full crouch

33. Suppose that, of 14 men assigned to a shop, 3 are absent. The percentage of men absent is, *most nearly,*

    A. 19%   B. 20%   C. 21%   D. 22%

34. The sum of 5 1/6 + 7 1/3 + 4 1/2 + 3 1/8 is

    A. 19 7/8   B. 20 1/2   C. 20 3/4   D. 20 7/8

35. A foreman must order enough sod to cover a dirt area 36 feet wide by 28 feet long. Each piece of sod is 3 feet long by 12 inches wide.
How many pieces of sod should be ordered to cover that area?

    A. 192   B. 236   C. 304   D. 336

36. If each man works at the same speed and 6 men take 2 1/2 hours to do a particular job, how many men will it take to do the *same* job in 1 hour?

    A. 13   B. 15   C. 26   D. 30

37. An agency bought 115 hammers from Company A for $253.00. It later bought 80 hammers from Company B for $140.00 If the agency had bought all of its hammers from Company B, the TOTAL AMOUNT of money that would have been *saved* would have been

    A. $25.25   B. $45.00   C. $51.75   D. $63.25

38. In order to make up a particular mixture of concrete, a foreman mixes 2 parts of cement to 3 parts of sand and 4 parts of gravel.
If he wants to make up 405 lbs. of concrete, he would need

    A. 45 lbs. of cement, 170 lbs. of sand, and 190 lbs. of gravel
    B. 45 lbs, of cement, 160 lbs. of sand, and 200 lbs. of gravel
    C. 90 lbs. of cement, 140 lbs. of sand, and 175 lbs. of gravel
    D. 90 lbs. of cement, 135 lbs. of sand, and 180 lbs. of gravel

39. A tank that is 5/8 full is holding 200 gallons of gasoline. The amount of gasoline this tank can hold *when filled* to capacity is

    A. 270 gals.   B. 320 gals.   C. 360 gals.   D. 410 gals.

40.

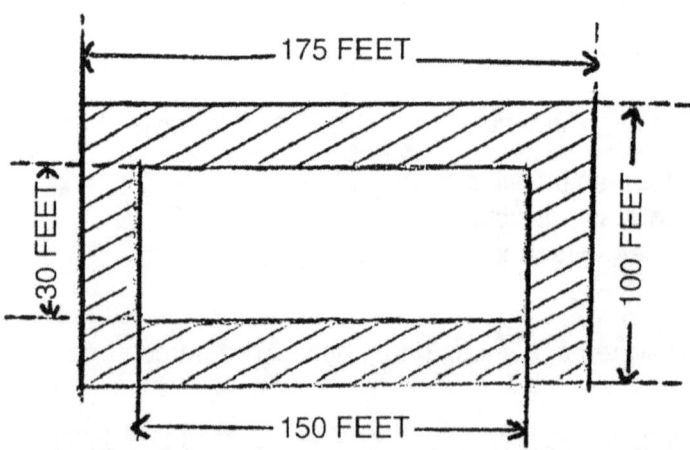

The shaded portion of the above drawing represents an icy walk surrounding a building. If it takes 1 lb. of rock salt to clear ice from every 100 square feet of walk, how many pounds of rock salt would be needed to clear the *entire* walk?

    A. 55   B. 60   C. 120   D. 175

KEY (CORRECT ANSWERS)

1.	C	11.	C	21.	D	31.	B
2.	A	12.	D	22.	C	32.	B
3.	A	13.	A	23.	B	33.	C
4.	B	14.	A	24.	C	34.	A
5.	D	15.	B	25.	B	35.	D
6.	C	16.	C	26.	C	36.	B
7.	C	17.	B	27.	A	37.	C
8.	B	18.	A	28.	C	38.	D
9.	D	19.	D	29.	D	39.	B
10.	C	20.	D	30.	B	40.	A

EXAMINATION SECTION
TEST 1

DIRECTIONS: Each question or incomplete statement is followed by several suggested answers or completions. Select the one that BEST answers the question or completes the statement. *PRINT THE LETTER OF THE CORRECT ANSWER IN THE SPACE AT THE RIGHT.*

1. Assume that the ticket agent at the bathhouse cannot dispense tickets from his machine because of a mechanical failure.
   You should authorize the ticket agent to

   A. sell tickets by hand from the bundle only
   B. stop selling tickets and await the installation of a stand-by machine
   C. collect cash from the patrons and have them escorted through the bathhouse entrance gate
   D. let the patrons deposit admission fees in a box at the bathhouse entrance gate

   1.____

2. If an operator of a four-wheel drive beach buggy leaves the sand portion of a beach and neglects to disengage his forward gears when he starts to drive over area streets to the dump or drop area, he will

   A. cause his transmission to lose linkage
   B. excessively wear his emergency brake
   C. jam up his front differential
   D. seriously damage the springs of the vehicle

   2.____

3. Inventories and replacement of material, supplies, and equipment required for pre-season preparation of beaches is normally scheduled to begin immediately after

   A. April 1st   B. Memorial Day
   C. Labor Day   D. New Year's Day

   3.____

4. On an Emerson Resuscitator, the cylinder is considered full when the cylinder volume indicator shows AT LEAST _____ lbs. pressure per square inch or more.

   A. 900   B. 1300   C. 1800   D. 2800

   4.____

5. The term *deadman,* when used in training courses for lifeguards assigned to oceanfront beaches, refers to

   A. a rope splicing tool
   B. beach cradles
   C. upland anchorage
   D. a fixed warning sign on a stone jetty

   5.____

6. The appropriate arm signal for a lifeguard to give from a standing position on his tower to call for delivery of a resuscitator is:

   A. Pump one arm up and down from an overhead position
   B. Rotary motion in front of chest
   C. Arms extended up -- straight overhead
   D. Arms clasped overhead

   6.____

7. The standard technique for executing the back pressure - arm lift method of artificial respiration requires the operator to adhere to a cycle consisting of a prescribed series of motions.
   This cycle should be repeated about _____ times per minute.

   A. two   B. four   C. six   D. twelve

8. Assume that an elderly swimmer has collapsed while swimming. His friend, who is with him, states that the victim has a long history of heart failure. The victim is brought to the first aid station showing signs of shock and labored breathing.
   You should take which one of the following actions?

   A. Apply an oxygen mask tightly to the victim's face
   B. Using the resuscitator, turn on the inhalator valve and apply the face mask
   C. Get him dressed and send him to a hospital with his friend
   D. Wrap him in blankets to keep warm and give him a hot beverage

9. The symptoms of heat prostration MOST usually are:

   A. Face pale, pulse weak; perspiration profuse on forehead, face, and hands; faintness and nausea
   B. Face red, hot, and dry; pulse strong and fast, high fever; perhaps nausea
   C. Face purplish; pulse erratic; feet and hands cold
   D. Face pale; respiration rate down to six; patient violent

10. Of the following, the BEST method for controlling algae growth in outdoor swimming pools is to

    A. treat with heavy dosages of chlorine
    B. raise the pH with additional amounts of calcium carbonate
    C. apply standard rates of copper sulphate
    D. lower the pool level and add fresh water from the main

11. To improve the capabilities of swimming pool filters, a jelly-like substance called a *flock* must be deposited on the surface of the filter bed.
    The flock is formed by adding which of the following two chemicals to the water in the treatment tank?

    A. Anhydrous ammonia and sodium dichromate
    B. Aluminum sulphate and sodium carbonate
    C. Orthotolidine and copper sulphate
    D. Iodides and calcium chloride

12. Pool water returning from the center drain of an outdoor swimming pool is called the

    A. confluent   B. effluent   C. influent   D. affluent

13. Backwashing in a conventional water treatment plant is USUALLY performed by the plant operator when the loss of head reaches _____ pounds per square inch.

    A. 3 1/2-4   B. 5 1/2-7   C. 8-10   D. 11-12

14. Most outdoor swimming pool operations have large heating boilers. These boilers have water columns with look-through water gauges, showing the water level in the boiler. The manual on maintenance and operation of heating plants and auxiliary equipment specifies that, while the boiler is in operation, the water column and gauge glass should be blown down   14._____

    A. daily   B. weekly   C. bi-weekly   D. monthly

15. Conventional gun-type oil burners used at park facilities are required to utilize as fuel   15._____

    A. #2 oil   B. #4 oil
    C. #6 oil   D. a kerosene mixture

16. Chlorine residual in municipally operated pools as required by the department of health shall be kept at NOT LESS THAN _____ ppm.   16._____

    A. 0.01   B. 0.25   C. 0.45   D. 1.0

17. Which of the following should be used to test the pH range (alkaline range) of swimming pool water?   17._____

    A. Ultraviolet light   B. Iodides
    C. Orthotolodine   D. Bromthymol blue

18. The filtration rate per square foot for a conventional filter is _____ gallons per square foot.   18._____

    A. 8   B. 6   C. 5   D. 3

19. Chlorine gas in steel cylinders is used as a sterilant in most outdoor swimming pools. If chlorine gas leaks occur from faulty connections, valve packings, etc., the STANDARD procedure for locating the leaks promptly is to use   19._____

    A. a lighted sulphur taper
    B. a soapy mixture
    C. acetone, applied with a camel hair brush
    D. concentrated ammonia

20. The MOST desirable time to apply lime to fairways on a golf course that is high in the acid range is   20._____

    A. during the rainy season   B. after a long, dry spell
    C. in the fall or spring   D. in late January

21. A bag of commercial fertilizer with a 10-6-4 classification on the printed face of the bag contains which of the following combination of chemicals by weight?   21._____

    A. 10% phosphoric acid, 6% nitrogen, and 4% potash
    B. 10% potash, 6% phosphoric acid, and 4% nitrogen
    C. 10% nitrogen, 6% phosphoric acid, and 4% potash
    D. 10% potash, 6% nitrogen, and 4% phosphoric acid

22. The turf on a tee with 15,000 square feet is badly worn because of traffic density and must be completely rehabilitated. You have completed the step requiring the application of a soil sterilant, and you are ready to apply nitrogen to the soil at a rate of two pounds of available nitrogen per thousand square feet.
   How many 100 pound bags of 10-6-4 fertilizer must be applied to adequately supply the nitrogen requirements?

   A. 10　　　B. 8　　　C. 5　　　D. 3

23. According to regulations relating to lawn-making, which of the following pH ratings of fertilizer is desirable?

   A. 4.5 to 5.0　　　B. 5.5 to 6.0
   C. 6.5 to 7.0　　　D. 7.5 to 8.0

24. To facilitate photosynthesis for normal growth, grass should be mowed often enough so that clippings are

   A. equal to mowing height
   B. shorter than mowing height
   C. longer than mowing height
   D. two inches long

25. Of the following, the MOST suitable grass seed mixture for a play field is one containing Kentucky bluegrass and

   A. colonial bent　　　B. Bermuda grass
   C. zoysia　　　D. creeping red fescue

26. Red fescue is USUALLY added to a seed mixture because of its

   A. drought resistance　　　B. fast germination
   C. slow germination　　　D. coarse texture

27. The four basic procedures generally considered as constituting the minimum maintenance for turf are: (1) selection of adapted grasses; (2) fertilization; (3) watering; and (4)

   A. aerification　　　B. mowing
   C. plugging　　　D. rolling

28. The BEST method for improving the soil structure of a heavily compacted playfield is to apply organic top-dressing first and then proceed with

   A. pesticide application　　　B. mowing and watering
   C. fertilization　　　D. aerification

29. A fairway should be maintained so that its width averages _____ to _____ feet.

   A. 60; 110　　　B. 120; 210　　　C. 220; 260　　　D. 270; 310

30. A good supplemental program to aid the grass that is already growing and to establish new grass in the thin, worn-out areas of an athletic field is

   A. overseeding　　　B. rolling
   C. plugging　　　D. watering

KEY (CORRECT ANSWERS)

1.	A	11.	B	21.	C
2.	C	12.	B	22.	D
3.	C	13.	B	23.	C
4.	C	14.	A	24.	B
5.	C	15.	A	25.	D
6.	C	16.	D	26.	A
7.	D	17.	D	27.	B
8.	B	18.	D	28.	D
9.	A	19.	D	29.	B
10.	C	20.	C	30.	A

TEST 2

DIRECTIONS: Each question or incomplete statement is followed by several suggested answers or completions. Select the one that BEST answers the question or completes the statement. *PRINT THE LETTER OF THE CORRECT ANSWER IN THE SPACE AT THE RIGHT.*

1. Traps are customarily surfaced with a layer of sand about _____ inches deep. 1.____
   A. 6   B. 12   C. 18   D. 24

2. A GOOD medium sandy loam for a putting green should contain _____ organic content. 2.____
   A. 5-10%   B. 10-15%   C. 20-30%   D. 30-50%

3. In the maintenance of a putting green, the LEAST necessary piece of equipment is 3.____
   A. putting green mower
   B. power sprayer
   C. aerator
   D. fertilizer spreader

4. The BEST way to maintain a green so that it holds a pitched ball is by 4.____
   A. overwatering
   B. good soil structure
   C. underwatering
   D. high mowing

5. The surface soil on a green should be a medium sandy loam placed _____ to _____ inches deep. 5.____
   A. 2; 4   B. 4; 6   C. 8; 10   D. 12; 18

6. The BEST turf fertilizers today contain about 6.____
   A. 85% slow-release phosphorus
   B. 16% fast-release nitrogen
   C. 50% slow-release nitrogen
   D. 20% phosphorus

7. Since golf course grasses are heavy users of phosphorus, potassium, magnesium, and calcium, the BEST pH range for turf, where maximum quantities of these chemicals are available, is 7.____
   A. 4.2 to 4.8
   B. 5.0 to 5.8
   C. 6.0 to 7.0
   D. 7.2 to 8.2

8. Damage on golf greens and other turf areas caused by the *Fusarium nivale* fungus (snow mold) can BEST be prevented or adequately checked by treatment with 8.____
   A. ammonium methyl arsenates
   B. aluminum sulphate
   C. hydrated lime
   D. cadminates

9. To prevent snow mold, treatment should GENERALLY start 9.____
   A. in early spring
   B. after a heavy rain
   C. in late winter
   D. after a heavy snow

10. Chlordane is used in turf management to

    A. eradicate goose grass
    B. control brown patch
    C. grub-proof soil
    D. stimulate root growth

11. Artificial rinks have refrigerants to cool the brine which is constantly circulated through the wrought-iron pipes imbedded in the floor of the rink.
    The brine can be chilled to below zero degrees Fahrenheit because it contains a chemical salt known as

    A. sodium chloride
    B. calcium chloride
    C. calcium carbonate
    D. ammonium chloride

12. The MINIMUM ice thickness generally considered safe for ice skating on a lake or pond whose depth does not exceed 3 feet is _____ inches.

    A. 2   B. 3   C. 5   D. 6

13. In the operation of an ice skating rink, prior to starting the process of ice building, the slab surface should be painted with _____ paint.

    A. white water
    B. white epoxy
    C. blue water
    D. blue epoxy

14. Crowd control in an ice skating rink includes all phases of the patrons' activities from admissions line-up to the time the patrons leave the rink.
    According to regulations, during special sessions, guards should

    A. skate in a clockwise direction
    B. skate in a counterclockwise direction
    C. be positioned on the ice near the entrances
    D. be positioned off the ice near the entrances

15. When a rink slab has been chilled below freezing temperature, ice can be built to the desired thickness by spraying a fine layer of water onto the slab with a

    A. Toro sprayer
    B. Skinner sprinkler
    C. Rainboni
    D. Zamboni

16. The following is a description of the cooling system of a skating rink: The refrigerant (ammonia or freon) absorbs the heat from the circulating brine which, in turn, lowers the temperature of the skating slab; when the brine is returned to the chiller after leaving the rink floor with absorbed heat, the compressor pumps the refrigerant gases to the condenser.
    The condenser does which of the following?
    It

    A. cools the refrigerant gas to a liquid and returns it to the chiller
    B. heats up the refrigerant gas
    C. transforms the gas into ice crystals
    D. cools the circulating water within the condenser

17. At indoor rinks where atmospheric temperatures remain stable and are not affected by outdoor weather conditions, brine should be circulated at a temperature of APPROXIMATELY _____ degrees Fahrenheit.

    A. 7   B. 10   C. 15   D. 25

18. Conditioning ice surfaces on outdoor rinks in early fall or late spring is BEST accomplished

    A. after each session
    B. after the sun sets
    C. at 8 A.M.
    D. at 12 noon

19. The standard of thickness for safe skating on lakes and ponds with water depths over three feet is _____ inches.

    A. two   B. three   C. five   D. seven

20. Assume that a heavy snowstorm has reached the area at the start of the evening session of outdoor rink operations. The one of the following actions that should be taken is to

    A. send all the skaters home, telling them the rink is closed
    B. let them skate until the snow is too deep to move
    C. cone off one-half of the rink at a time for snow removal operations
    D. give snow shovels to as many skaters as possible and put them to work clearing the rink

21. Of the following trees, the one which is NOT recommended for street tree planting is

    A. London plane   B. Gingko
    C. Yellow Pine   D. Pin Oak

22. Before useful measures can be applied to control a tree disease epidemic in a park, it is FIRST necessary to

    A. obtain an appropriation for spraying
    B. have a correct diagnosis made of the disease
    C. make an inventory of the diseased trees
    D. wait until winter when the trees are dormant

23. Of the following trees, the one which is generally MOST often recommended for sandy soils is

    A. American elm   B. Japanese maple
    C. Chinese poplar   D. Japanese black pine

24. About 75 percent of all tree diseases, including all mildews, rusts, anthracnoses, and sooty molds, are caused by

    A. fungi   B. viruses   C. nematodes   D. bacteria

25. Tree crews should be instructed to ALWAYS

    A. trim the leader of a tree to improve its vitality
    B. prune trees by removing at least 50% of the crowns
    C. remove all injured and diseased wood
    D. fertilize a tree before pruning it

26. Three techniques that you can use to evaluate maintenance activities and determine whether they can be done better are work simplification, work measurement, and 26.____

   A. establishment of work performance standards
   B. use of labor saving devices
   C. increased supervision
   D. computerization

27. Staffing is BEST indicated by which of the following activities? 27.____

   A. Selection and training of personnel and maintaining favorable conditions of work
   B. Structuring an organization for unity of command, span of control, and lines of authority
   C. Writing task lists for the different titles working at a facility
   D. Working out in broad outline the things that need to be done and the methods for doing them to accomplish the mission of the agency

28. Generally, the MOST practical way to ascertain most readily the number of man-hours it takes to do a job is by 28.____

   A. referring to a management analysis handbook
   B. making a detailed analysis of the job
   C. asking the operator performing the job
   D. reviewing job specifications

29. Any violation of the rules or regulations for the government and protection of public parks and property shall be punishable by NOT MORE THAN _____ imprisonment or by a fine of not more than _____ dollars, or by both. 29.____

   A. thirty days'; fifty
   B. sixty days'; one hundred
   C. ninety days'; two hundred fifty
   D. one year's; five hundred

30. One workman can hand-rake leaves at the rate of approximately 1,000 square feet in 20 minutes. 30.____
   How many men would you assign to a crew to hand rake a grove of trees covering 40,000 square feet in order to accomplish the job within three hours?

   A. 3   B. 30   C. 50   D. 5

KEY (CORRECT ANSWERS)

1.	A	11.	B	21.	C
2.	C	12.	B	22.	B
3.	B	13.	A	23.	D
4.	B	14.	D	24.	A
5.	C	15.	D	25.	C
6.	C	16.	A	26.	A
7.	C	17.	C	27.	A
8.	D	18.	A	28.	C
9.	A	19.	C	29.	A
10.	C	20.	C	30.	D

EXAMINATION SECTION
TEST 1

DIRECTIONS: Each question or incomplete statement is followed by several suggested answers or completions. Select the one that BEST answers the question or completes the statement. *PRINT THE LETTER OF THE CORRECT ANSWER IN THE SPACE AT THE RIGHT.*

Questions 1-3.

DIRECTIONS: Questions 1 through 3, inclusive, are to be answered in accordance with the American Standard Graphical Symbols for Pipe Fittings, Valves, and Piping and American Standard Graphical Symbols for Heating, Ventilating and Air Conditioning.

1. The symbol shown on a piping drawing represents a _____ elbow.

   A. turned down
   B. reducing
   C. long radius
   D. turned up

2. The symbol shown on a heating drawing represents a(n)

   A. expansion joint
   B. hanger or support
   C. heat exchanger
   D. air eliminator

3. The symbol shown on a piping drawing represents a _____ gate valve.

   A. welded
   B. flanged
   C. screwed
   D. bell and spigot

4. The MAIN purpose for the inspection of plant equipment, buildings, and facilities is to

   A. determine the quality of maintenance work of all the trades
   B. prevent the overstocking of equipment and materials used in maintenance work
   C. forecast normal maintenance jobs for existing equipment, buildings, and facilities
   D. prevent unscheduled interruptions of operating equipment and excessive deterioration of buildings and facilities

5. Of the following devices, the one that is used to determine the rating, in cubic feet per minute, of a unit ventilator is a(n)

   A. psychrometer
   B. pyrometer
   C. anemometer
   D. manometer

6. A number of 4' x 6' skids loaded with material are to be stored. Assume that the total weight of each loaded skid is 1200 pounds and that the maximum allowable floor load is 280 lbs. per sq. ft.
   The MAXIMUM number of skids that can be stacked vertically without exceeding the MAXIMUM allowable floor load is

   A. 4
   B. 5
   C. 6
   D. 7

7. Specifications which contain the term *slump test* would MOST likely refer to

   A. lumber B. paint C. concrete D. water

8. Of the following sizes of copper conductors, the one which has the LEAST current-carrying capacity is _____ AWG.

   A. 000 B. 0 C. 8 D. 12

9. The size of a steel beam is shown on a steel drawing as W 8 x 15.
   In accordance with the latest edition of the Steel Construction Manual of the American Institute of Steel Construction, the number 8 in W 8 x 15 represents the beam's *approximate*

   A. depth
   B. flange thickness
   C. width
   D. web thickness

10. For expediting control functions such as work methods, planning, scheduling, and work measurement, EQUIPMENT RECORDS must contain specific data.
    Of the following, the data which is NOT usually indicated on an EQUIPMENT RECORD card is

    A. machinery and parts specifications numbers
    B. a breakdown history
    C. a preventive maintenance history
    D. salvage value on the open market

11. Refrigeration piping, valves, fittings, and related parts used in the construction and installation of refrigeration systems shall conform to the

    A. American Society of Mechanical Engineers Boiler and Pressure Vessel Code
    B. American Standards Association Code for Pressure Piping
    C. Pipe Fabrication Institute Standards
    D. Underwriters Laboratory Standards

12. The maintenance term *downtime* means MOST NEARLY the

    A. period of time in which a machine is out of service
    B. routine replacement of parts or materials to a piece of equipment
    C. labor required for clean-up of equipment to insure its proper operation
    D. maintenance work which is confined to checking, adjusting, and lubrication of equipment

13. A supplier quotes a list price of $172.00 less 15 and 10 percent for twelve tools.
    The ACTUAL cost for these twelve tools is MOST NEARLY

    A. $146 B. $132 C. $129 D. $112

14. Of the following colors of electrical conductor coverings, the one which indicates a conductor used SOLELY for grounding portable or fixed electrical equipment is

    A. blue B. green C. red D. black

15. A *medium duty* type of scaffold is one on which the working load on the platform surface must NOT exceed _____ pounds per square foot.

    A. 50 B. 70 C. 90 D. 110

16. Assume that a mechanic is using a powder-actuated tool and the cartridge misfires. According to recommended safe practices regarding a misfired cartridge, the FIRST course of action the mechanic should take is to

    A. place the misfired cartridge carefully into a metal container filled with water
    B. carefully reload the tool with the misfired cartridge and try it again
    C. immediately bury the misfired cartridge at least two feet in the ground
    D. remove the wadding from the misfired cartridge and empty the powder into a pail of sand

16.____

17. The ratings used in classifying fire resistant building construction materials are MOST frequently expressed in

    A. Btu's   B. hours   C. temperatures   D. pounds

17.____

18. The only legible portion of the nameplate on a piece of equipment reads: *208 volts, 3 phase, 10 H.P.*
    This data would MOST NEARLY indicate that the piece of equipment is a(n)

    A. amplifier   B. fixture ballast
    C. motor   D. rectifier

18.____

19. Of the following items relating to the maintenance of roofs, the one which is of the LEAST value in a preventive maintenance program for roofs is knowledge of the

    A. roofing specifications   B. application procedures
    C. process of deterioration   D. frequency of rainstorms

19.____

20. In an oxyacetylene cutting outfit, the color of the hose that is connected to the oxygen cylinder is USUALLY

    A. white   B. yellow   C. red   D. green

20.____

21. Assume that a welding generator is to be used to weld partitions made of 18 gauge steel. Of the following settings, the BEST one to use would be a _____ setting of voltage and a _____ setting of amperage.

    A. high; high   B. high; low   C. low; high   D. low; low

21.____

22. According to the administrative code, when color marking is used, potable water lines shall be painted

    A. yellow   B. blue   C. red   D. green

22.____

23. A set of mechanical plan drawings is drawn to a scale of 1/8" = 1 foot.
    If a length of pipe measures 15 7/16" on the drawing, the ACTUAL length of the pipe is _____ feet.

    A. 121.5   B. 122.5   C. 123.5   D. 124.5

23.____

24. A portion of a specification states: *Concrete, other than that placed under water, should be compacted and worked into place by spading or puddling.*
    The MAIN reason why *spading and puddling* is required is to

    A. insure that all water in the concrete mix is brought to the surface
    B. eliminate stone pockets and large bubbles of air

24.____

C. provide a means to obtain a spade full of concrete for test purposes
D. make allowances for *bleeding and segregation* of the concrete

25. Assume that the following statement appears in a construction contract: *Payment will be made for the number of pounds of bar reinforcement incorporated in the work as shown on the plans.*
    This type of contract is MOST likely

    A. cost plus   B. lump sum   C. subcontract   D. unit price

26. Partial payments to outside contractors are USUALLY based on the

    A. breakdown estimate submitted after the contract was signed
    B. actual cost of labor and material plus overhead and profit
    C. estimate of work completed which is generally submitted periodically
    D. estimate of material delivered to the job

27. Building contracts usually require that estimates for changes made in the field be submitted for approval before the work can start.
    The MAIN reason for this requirement is to

    A. make sure that the contractor understands the change
    B. discourage such changes
    C. keep the contractor honest
    D. enable the department to control its expenses

28. An *addendum* to contract specifications means MOST NEARLY

    A. a substantial completion payment to the contractor for work almost completed
    B. final acceptance of the work by authorities of all contract work still to be done
    C. additional contract provisions issued in writing by authorities prior to receipt of bids
    D. work other than that required by the contract at the time of its execution

29. Of the following terms, the one which is usually NOT used to describe the types of payments to outside contractors for work done is the _____ payment.

    A. partial payment   B. substantial completion
    C. final   D. surety

30. Of the following metals, the one which is a ferrous metal is

    A. cast iron   B. brass   C. bronze   D. babbit

31. Assume that you have assigned six mechanics to do a job that must be finished in four days. At the end of three days, your men have completed only two-thirds of the job. In order to complete the job on time and because the job is such that it cannot be speeded up, you should assign a MINIMUM of _____ extra men.

    A. 3   B. 4   C. 5   D. 6

32. Of the following traps, the one which is NORMALLY used to retain steam in a heating unit or piping is the _____ trap.

    A. P   B. running   C. float   D. bell

33. Of the following materials, the one which is a convenient and powerful adhesive for cementing tears in canvas jackets that are wrapped around warm pipe insulation is   33.____

   A. cylinder oil B. wheat paste
   C. water glass D. latex paint

34. Pipe chases should be provided with an access door PRIMARILY to provide means to   34.____

   A. replace piping lines
   B. either inspect or manipulate valves
   C. prevent condensate from forming on the pipes
   D. check the chase for possible structural defects

35. Electric power is measured in   35.____

   A. volts   B. amperes   C. watts   D. ohms

KEY (CORRECT ANSWERS)

1.	D	16.	A
2.	A	17.	B
3.	B	18.	C
4.	D	19.	D
5.	C	20.	D
6.	B	21.	B
7.	C	22.	D
8.	D	23.	C
9.	A	24.	B
10.	D	25.	D
11.	B	26.	C
12.	A	27.	D
13.	B	28.	C
14.	B	29.	D
15.	A	30.	A

31. A
32. C
33. C
34. B
35. C

TEST 2

DIRECTIONS: Each question or incomplete statement is followed by several suggested answers or completions. Select the one that BEST answers the question or completes the statement. *PRINT THE LETTER OF THE CORRECT ANSWER IN THE SPACE AT THE RIGHT.*

1. The HIGHEST quality tools should   1.___

    A. always be bought
    B. never be bought
    C. be bought when they offer an overall advantage
    D. be bought only for foreman

2. Master keys should have no markings that will identify them as such.   2.___
   This statement is

    A. *false;* it would be impossible to keep records about them without such markings
    B. *true;* markings are subject to alteration and vandalization
    C. *false;* without such markings, they would be too lightly regarded by those to whom issued
    D. *true;* markings would only highlight their value to a potential wrongdoer

3. For a foreman to usually delay for a few weeks handling grievances his men make is a   3.___

    A. *poor* practice; it can affect the morale of the men
    B. *good* practice; it will discourage grievances
    C. *poor* practice; the causes of grievances usually disappear if action is delayed
    D. *good* practice; most employee grievances are not justified

4. Whenever an important change in procedure is contemplated, some foremen make a point of discussing the matter with their subordinates in order to get their viewpoint on the proposed change.   4.___
   In general, this practice is advisable MAINLY for the reason that

    A. subordinates can often see the effects of procedural changes more clearly than foremen
    B. the foreman has an opportunity to explain the advantages of the new procedure
    C. future changes will be welcomed if subordinates are kept informed
    D. participation in work planning helps to build a spirit of cooperation among employees

5. An estimate of employee morale could LEAST effectively be appraised by   5.___

    A. checking accident and absenteeism records
    B. determining the attitudes of employees toward their job
    C. examining the number of requests for emergency leaves of absence
    D. reviewing the number and nature of employee suggestions

6. Assume that you are a foreman and that a visitor at the job site asks you what your crew is doing.   6.___
   You should

A. respectfully decline to answer since all questions must be answered by the proper authority
B. answer as concisely as possible but discourage undue conversation
C. refer the man to your superiors
D. give the person complete details of the job

7. Cooperation can BEST be obtained from the general public by

   A. siding with them whenever they have a complaint
   B. sticking carefully to your work and ignoring everything else
   C. explaining the department's objectives and why the public must occasionally be temporarily inconvenienced
   D. listening politely to their complaints and telling them that the complaints will be forwarded to the main office

8. While you are working for the city, a man says to you that one of the rules of your job doesn't make sense and he gets mad.
   You should say to him

   A. Leave me alone so I can get my work done
   B. Everyone must follow the rules
   C. Let me tell you the reason for the rule
   D. I'm only doing my job so don't get mad at me

9. One approach to preparing written reports to superiors is to present first the conclusions and recommendations and then the data on which the conclusions and recommendations are based.
   The use of this approach is BEST justified when the

   A. data completely support the conclusions and recommendations
   B. superiors lack the specific training and experience required to understand and interpret the data
   C. data contain more information than is required for making the conclusions and recommendations
   D. superiors are more interested in the conclusions and recommendations than in the data

10. The MOST important reason why separate paragraphs might be used in writing a report is that this

    A. makes it easier to understand the report
    B. permits the report to be condensed
    C. gives a better appearance to the report
    D. prevents accidental elimination of important facts

11. On a drawing, the following standard cross-section represents MOST NEARLY

    A. sand   B. concrete   C. earth   D. rock

12. On a drawing, the following standard cross-section represents MOST NEARLY

    A. malleable iron   B. steel
    C. bronze   D. lead

13. On a piping plan drawing, the symbol represents a 90° _____ elbow.

    A. flanged   B. screwed
    C. bell and spigot D. welded

14. On a drawing, the symbol represents

    A. stone   B. steel   C. glass   D. wood

15. On a heating piping drawing, the symbol _____ represents piping.

    A. high-pressure steam   B. medium-pressure steam
    C. low-pressure   D. hot water supply

16. Of the following devices, the one that is LEAST frequently used to attach a piece of equipment to concrete or masonry walls is a(n)

    A. carriage bolt   B. through bolt
    C. lag screw   D. expansion bolt

17. A vapor barrier is usually installed in conjunction with

    A. drainage piping   B. roof flashing
    C. building insulation D. wood sheathing

Questions 18-20.

DIRECTIONS: Questions 18 through 20 are to be answered in accordance with the following table

	Man Days Borough 1 Oct. Nov.	Man Days Borough 2 Oct. Nov.	Man Days Borough 3 Oct. Nov.	Man Days Borough 4 Oct. Nov.
Carpenter	70 100	35 180	145 205	120 85
Plumber	95 135	195 100	70 130	135 80
House Painter	90 90	120 80	85 85	95 195
Electrician	120 110	135 155	120 95	70 205
Blacksmith	125 145	60 180	205 145	80 125

18. In accordance with the above table, if the average daily pay of the five trades listed above is $47.50, the approximate labor cost of work done by the five trades during the month of October for Borough 1 is MOST NEARLY

    A. $22,800   B. $23,450   C. $23,750   D. $26,125

4 (#2)

19. In accordance with the above table, the Borough which MOST NEARLY made up 22.4% of the total plumbing work force for the month of November is Borough   19.____

    A. 1   B. 2   C. 3   D. 4

20. In accordance with the above table, the average man days per month per Borough spent on electrical work for all Boroughs combined is MOST NEARLY   20.____

    A. 120   B. 126   C. 130   D. 136

21. Of the following percentages of carbon, the one that would indicate a medium carbon steel is   21.____

    A. 0.2%   B. 0.4%   C. 0.8%   D. 1.2%

22. A *screw pitch gage* measures only the   22.____

    A. looseness of threads
    B. tightness of threads
    C. number of threads per inch
    D. gage number

23. Assume that you are to make an inspection of a building to determine the need for painting.   23.____
Of the following tools, the one which is LEAST needed to aid you in your inspection is a

    A. sharp penknife   B. putty knife
    C. lightweight tack hammer   D. six-foot rule

24. A *slump test* for concrete is used MAINLY to measure the concrete's   24.____

    A. strength   B. consistency   C. flexibility   D. porosity

25. Specifications which contain the term *kiln dried* would MOST likely refer to   25.____

    A. asphalt shingles   B. brick veneer
    C. paint lacquer   D. lumber

26. In accordance with established jurisdictional work procedures among the trades, the person you would assign to replace a malfunctioning fire sprinkler head would be a   26.____

    A. plumber   B. laborer   C. housesmith   D. steamfitter

27. Of the following types of union shops, the one which is illegal under the Taft-Hartley Law is the _____ shop.   27.____

    A. closed   B. open
    C. union   D. union representative

28. Of the following types of contracts, the one that in city work would MOST likely be limited to emergency work *only* is   28.____

    A. lump-sum
    B. unit-price
    C. cost-plus
    D. partial cost-plus and lump-sum

29. Of the following qualifications of outside work contractors, the one which is the LEAST important requirement for determining eligible contractors is

   A. availability
   B. size of work force
   C. experience
   D. location of business

30. Of the following piping materials, the one that combines the physical strength of mild steel with the corrosion resistance of gray iron is

   A. grade A steel
   B. grey cast iron
   C. welded wrought iron
   D. ductile iron

31. Assume that a can of red lead paint needs to be thinned slightly. Of the following, the one that should be used is

   A. turpentine
   B. lacquer thinner
   C. water
   D. alcohol

32. Assume that a trench is 42" wide, 5' deep, and 100' long. If the unit price of excavating the trench is $35 per cubic yard, the cost of excavating the trench is MOST NEARLY

   A. $2,275   B. $5,110   C. $7,000   D. $21,000

33. Of the following uses, the one for which a bituminous compound would usually be used is to

   A. prevent corrosion of burled steel tanks
   B. increase the strength of concrete
   C. caulk water pipes
   D. paint inside wood columns

34. An electrical drawing is drawn to a scale of 1/4" = 1'.
If a length of conduit on the drawing measures 7 3/8", the actual length of the conduit, in feet, is MOST NEARLY

   A. 7.5'   B. 15.5'   C. 22.5'   D. 29.5'

35. Of the following steam heating systems, the one that operates under both vacuum and low pressure conditions, without using a vacuum pump, is generally known as a _____ system.

   A. one pipe low pressure
   B. vacuum
   C. vapor
   D. high pressure

36. Of the following valve trim symbols, the one which designates a valve trim made of monel material is

   A. 8-18   B. NI-CU   C. SM   D. MI

37. A replacement part for a piece of equipment is to be made of S.A.E. 4047 steel. This material is MOST likely a _____ steel.

   A. wrought
   B. nickel
   C. chrome-vanadium
   D. molybdenum

38. A metallic underground water piping system is to be used as a means of grounding. Of the following statements concerning use of this system, the one that is MOST NEARLY CORRECT is that this use is

    A. not permitted
    B. permitted where available
    C. absolutely required
    D. permitted only in certain cases

39. For pipe sizes up to 8", schedule 40 pipe is identical to _____ pipe.

    A. standard
    B. extra strong
    C. double extra strong
    D. type M copper

40. Assume that a shop is undergoing a general housecleaning, and all excess unused materials have been removed. *Clean-up work,* as pertains to painting in this case, means MOST NEARLY

    A. a thorough two-coat paint job
    B. only that surface which was marred to be painted
    C. a one-coat job to *freshen things up*
    D. only that iron work is to be painted

41. The *United States Standard Gage* is used to measure sheet metal thicknesses of

    A. iron and steel
    B. aluminum
    C. copper
    D. tin

42. Headers and stretchers are used in the construction of

    A. floors   B. walls   C. ceilings   D. roofs

Questions 43-44.

DIRECTIONS: Questions 43 and 44, inclusive, are to be answered in accordance with the following paragraph.

For cast iron pipe lines, the middle ring or sleeve shall have <u>beveled</u> ends and shall be high quality cast iron. The middle ring shall have a minimum wall thickness of 3/8" for pipe up to 8", 7/16" for pipe 10" to 30", and 1/2" for pipe over 30", nominal diameter. Minimum length of middle ring shall be 5" for pipe up to 10", 6" for pipe 10" to 30", and 10" for pipe 30" nominal diameter and larger. The middle ring shall not have a center pipe stop, unless otherwise specified.

43. As used in the above paragraph, the word *beveled* means MOST NEARLY

    A. straight   B. slanted   C. curved   D. rounded

44. In accordance with the above paragraph, the middle ring of a 24" nominal diameter pipe would have a minimum wall thickness and length of _____ thick and _____ long.

    A. 3/8"; 5"   B. 3/8"; 6"   C. 7/16"; 6"   D. 1/2"; 6"

45. A work order is NOT usually issued for which one of the following jobs: 45.___

    A. Repairing wood door frames
    B. Taking daily inventory
    C. Installing electric switches in maintenance shop
    D. Repairing a number of valves in boiler room

46. Of the following statements, the one which usually does NOT pertain to preventative maintenance programs is 46.___

    A. periodic inspection of facilities
    B. lubrication of equipment
    C. minor repair of equipment
    D. complete replacement of deteriorated equipment

Questions 47-50.

DIRECTIONS: Questions 47 through 50, inclusive, are based on the sketch of metal sheet shown below. (Sketch not to scale.)

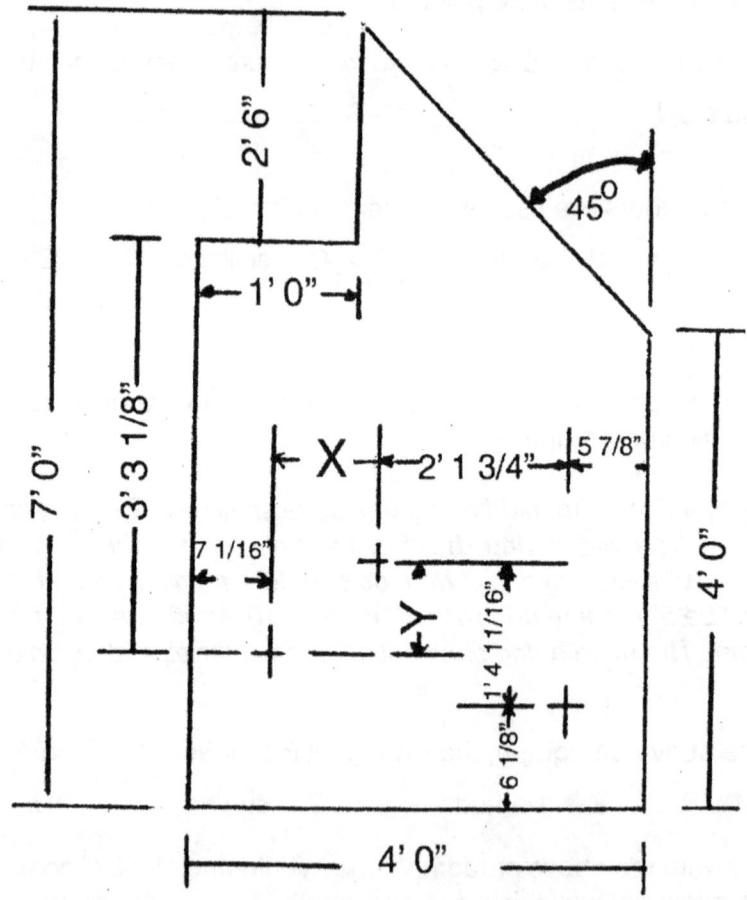

47. From the above sketch, the distance marked X is MOST NEARLY 47.___

    A. 5 1/4"   B. 6 5/16"   C. 7 1/8"   D. 9 5/16"

48. From the above sketch, the distance marked Y is MOST NEARLY

    A. 5 11/16"   B. 6 3/16"   C. 7 5/16"   D. 8 11/16"

49. In reference to the above sketch, if each piece is made from a rectangular piece of metal measuring 4' x 7', the percent of waste material is MOST NEARLY

    A. 10%   B. 15%   C. 25%   D. 30%

50. In reference to the above sketch, if the metal is 1/4" thick and weighs 144 pounds per cubic foot, the net weight of one piece would be MOST NEARLY _____ pounds.

    A. 51   B. 63   C. 75   D. 749

KEY (CORRECT ANSWERS)

1. C	11. A	21. B	31. A	41. A
2. D	12. C	22. C	32. A	42. B
3. A	13. A	23. D	33. A	43. B
4. D	14. D	24. B	34. D	44. C
5. C	15. B	25. D	35. C	45. B
6. B	16. A	26. D	36. B	46. D
7. C	17. C	27. A	37. D	47. D
8. C	18. C	28. C	38. B	48. D
9. D	19. B	29. D	39. A	49. C
10. A	20. B	30. D	40. C	50. B

EXAMINATION SECTION
TEST 1

DIRECTIONS: Each question or incomplete statement is followed by several suggested answers or completions. Select the one that BEST answers the question or completes the statement. *PRINT THE LETTER OF THE CORRECT ANSWER IN THE SPACE AT THE RIGHT.*

1. A maintenance man complains to you that he is getting all the boring jobs to do. You check and find that his complaint has no basis in fact.
   The one of the following which is the MOST likely reason why the maintenance man made such a claim is that he

   A. wants to get even with the supervisor
   B. lives in a world of fantasy
   C. believes the injustice to be real
   D. is jealous of other workers

   1.____

2. When on preliminary review of a mechanic's written grievance you feel the grievance to be unfounded, the FIRST step you should take is to

   A. show the mechanic where he is wrong
   B. check carefully to find out why the mechanic thinks that way
   C. try to humor the mechanic out of it
   D. tell the mechanic to stop complaining

   2.____

3. Assume that you decide to hold a private meeting with one of your mechanics who has a drinking problem that is affecting his work.
   At the meeting, the BEST way for you to handle this situation is to

   A. tell the mechanic off and then listen to what he has to say
   B. criticize the mechanic's behavior to get him to *open up* in order to help him correct his problem quickly
   C. try to get the mechanic to recognize his problem and find ways to solve it
   D. limit the discussion to matters concerning only the problem and look for immediate results

   3.____

4. The one of the following which is a generally accepted guide in criticizing a subordinate EFFECTIVELY is to

   A. criticize the improper act, not the individual
   B. put the listener on the defensive
   C. make the criticism general instead of specific
   D. correct the personality, not the situation

   4.____

5. The one of the following disciplinary methods by which you are MOST likely to be successful in getting a problem employee to improve his behavior is when you

   A. discipline the employee in front of others
   B. consider the matter to be ended after the disciplining
   C. give the exact same discipline no matter how serious the wrongdoing
   D. make an example of the employee

   5.____

6. Of the following statements, the one that is MOST applicable to a disciplinary situation is that discipline should be

    A. used after a cooling-off period
    B. identical for all employees
    C. consistent with the violation
    D. based on personal feelings

7. The one of the following approaches that is MOST important for you to take in evaluating a mechanic in order to increase his work productivity is to

    A. first have him evaluate his own performance
    B. meet with him to discuss how he is doing and what is expected on the job
    C. send him a copy of your evaluation of his work performance and give him the opportunity to submit written comments
    D. express in writing your appreciation of his work

8. Assume that you say to one of the mechanics, *Jim, that job you turned out today was top-notch. I didn't think you could do so well with the kind of material you had to work with.*
   This statement BEST describes an example of your

    A. recognition of the man's work
    B. disrespect for the man's feelings
    C. personal favoritism of the man
    D. constructive criticism of the man's work

9. In general, the OUTSTANDING characteristic of employees over 50 years of age is their

    A. resistance   B. endurance
    C. wisdom   D. job stability

10. You should be interested in the morale of your men because morale is MOST often associated with

    A. mechanization   B. automation
    C. production   D. seniority regulations

11. Assume that the maintenance work order system is about to be changed. Your workers would MOST likely show the LEAST resistance to this change if you

    A. downgrade the old maintenance work order system
    B. tell your workers how the change will benefit them
    C. post the notice of the change on the bulletin board
    D. tell the workers how the change will benefit management

12. Of the following, the BEST way to motivate a newly appointed mechanic is to

    A. explain the meaning of each assignment
    B. make the work more physically demanding
    C. test the mechanic's ability
    D. use as much authority as possible

13. The one of the following which is the LEAST important reason for giving employees information concerning policy changes which will affect them is that employees should know

    A. why the change is being made
    B. who will be affected by the change
    C. when the change will go into effect
    D. how much savings will be made by the change

14. A foreman who knows how to handle his men will MOST likely get them to produce more by treating them

    A. alike
    B. as individuals
    C. on a casual basis
    D. as a group

15. Of the following items, the one that a supervisor has the MOST right to expect from his employees is

    A. liking the job
    B. a fair day's work
    C. equal skill of all mechanics
    D. perfection

16. The one of the following which is the BEST practice for you to follow in handling a dispute between the workers is to

    A. side with one of the workers so as to end the dispute quickly
    B. pay no attention to the dispute and let the workers settle it themselves
    C. listen to each worker's story of the dispute and then decide how to settle it
    D. discuss the dispute with other workers and then decide how to settle it

17. You are likely to run into an employee morale problem when assigning a dirty job that comes up often.
    Of the following, the BEST method of assigning this work is to

    A. rotate this assignment
    B. assign it to the fastest worker
    C. assign it by seniority
    D. assign it to the least skilled worker

18. Of the following, the one that is generally regarded as the BEST aid to high work productivity of subordinates is a supervisor's skill in

    A. record keeping
    B. technical work
    C. setting up rules and regulations
    D. human relations

19. The BEST way to help a mechanic who comes to you for advice on a personal problem is to

    A. listen to the worker's problem without passing judgment
    B. tell the worker to forget about the problem and to stop letting it interfere with his work
    C. talk about your own personal problems to the worker
    D. mind your own business and leave the worker alone

20. You are in charge of the maintenance shop and have learned that within the next two weeks the maintenance shop will be moved to a new location on the plant grounds, but you have not learned why this move is taking place. Assume that you have decided not to keep this information from your mechanics until the reason is known but to inform them of this matter now.
Of the following, which one is the BEST argument that can be made regarding your decision?

    A. *Acceptable;* because although the reason is not now known, the mechanics will eventually find out about the move
    B. *Unacceptable;* because the mechanics do not know at this time the reason for the move and this will cause anxiety on their part
    C. *Acceptable*; because the mechanics will be affected by the move and they should be told what is happening
    D. *Unacceptable;* because the mechanics' advance knowledge of the move will tend to slow down their work output

21. Of the following, the FIRST action for a foreman to take in making a decision is to

    A. get all the facts
    B. develop alternate solutions
    C. get opinions of others
    D. know the results in advance

22. Assume that you have just been promoted to foreman.
Of the following, the BEST practice to follow regarding your previous experience at the mechanic's level is to

    A. continue to fraternize with your old friends
    B. use this experience to better understand those who now work for you
    C. use your old connections to keep top management informed of mechanics' views
    D. forget the mechanics' points of view

23. You have decided to hold regular group discussions with your subordinates on various aspects of their duties.
Of the following methods you might use to begin such a program, the one which is likely to be MOST productive is to

    A. express your own ideas and persuade the group to accept them
    B. save time and cover more ground by asking questions calling for yes or no answers
    C. propose to the group a general plan of action rather than specific ideas carefully worked out
    D. provide an informal atmosphere for the exchange of ideas

24. The principle of learning by which a foreman might get the BEST results in training his subordinates is:

    A. Letting the learner discover and correct his own mistakes
    B. Teaching the most technical part of the work first
    C. Teaching all parts of the work during the first training session
    D. Getting the learner to use as many of his five senses as possible

25. A new mechanic is to be trained to do an involved operation containing several steps of varying difficulty. This mechanic will MOST likely learn the operation more quickly if he is taught 25.____

    A. each step in its proper order
    B. the hardest steps first
    C. the easiest steps first
    D. first the steps that do not require tools

KEY (CORRECT ANSWERS)

1.	C	11.	B
2.	B	12.	A
3.	C	13.	D
4.	A	14.	B
5.	B	15.	B
6.	C	16.	C
7.	B	17.	A
8.	A	18.	D
9.	D	19.	A
10.	C	20.	C

21. A
22. B
23. D
24. D
25. C

TEST 2

DIRECTIONS: Each question or incomplete statement is followed by several suggested answers or completions. Select the one that BEST answers the question or completes the statement. *PRINT THE LETTER OF THE CORRECT ANSWER IN THE SPACE AT THE RIGHT.*

1. The one of the following job situations in which it is better to give a written order than an oral order is when 1.___

    A. the job involves many details
    B. you can check the job's progress easily
    C. the job is repetitive in nature
    D. there is an emergency

2. Which one of the following serves as the BEST guideline for you to follow for effective written reports? 2.___
Keep sentences

    A. short and limit sentences to one thought
    B. short and use as many thoughts as possible
    C. long and limit sentences to one thought
    D. long and use as many thoughts as possible

3. Of the following, the BEST reason why a foreman generally should not do the work of an individual mechanic is that 3.___

    A. the shop's production figures will not be accurate
    B. a foreman is paid to supervise
    C. the foreman must maintain his authority
    D. the employee may become self-conscious

4. One method by which a foreman might prepare written reports to management is to begin with the conclusions, results, or summary and to follow this with the supporting data. 4.___
The BEST reason why management may prefer this form of report is because

    A. management lacks the specific training to understand the data
    B. the data completely supports the conclusions
    C. time is saved by getting to the conclusions of the report first
    D. the data contains all the information that is required for making the conclusions

5. Forms used for time records and work orders are important to the work of a foreman PRIMARILY because they give him 5.___

    A. the knowledge of and familiarity with work operations
    B. the means of control of personnel, material, or job costs
    C. the means for communicating with other workers
    D. a useful method for making filing procedures easier

6. The one of the following which is the MOST important factor in determining the number of employees you can effectively supervise is the

   A. type of work to be performed
   B. priority of the work to be performed
   C. salary level of the workers
   D. ratio of permanent employees to temporary employees

   6._____

7. Of the following, you will be MOST productive in carrying out your supervisory responsibilities if you

   A. are capable of doing the same work as your mechanics
   B. meet with your mechanics frequently
   C. are very friendly with your mechanics
   D. get work done through your mechanics

   7._____

8. You have been asked to prepare the annual budget for your maintenance shop.
   The one of the following which is the FIRST step you should take in preparing this budget is to determine the

   A. amount of maintenance work which is scheduled for the shop
   B. time it takes for a specific unit of work to be completed
   C. current workload of each employee in the shop
   D. policies and procedures of the shop's operations

   8._____

9. When determining the amount of work you expect a group of mechanics to perform in a given time, the BEST procedure for you to follow should be to

   A. aim for a higher level of production than that of the most productive worker
   B. stay at the present production level
   C. set general instead of specific goals
   D. let workers participate in the determination whenever possible

   9._____

10. You have been asked to set next year's performance goals concerning the ratio of jobs completed on schedule to total jobs worked. A review of last year's record shows that the workers completed their jobs on schedule 85% of the time, with the best ones showing an on-time ratio of 92% and the poorest ones showing an on-time ratio of 65%.
    Using these facts in line with generally accepted goal-setting practices, you should set a performance ratio for the next year on the basis of _____ average with a _____ minimum acceptable for any employee.

    A. 85%; 65%   B. 85%; 70%   C. 90%; 65%   D. 90%; 70%

    10._____

11. It is important for you to be able to identify the critical parts of a large project such as the remodeling of your maintenance shop.
    The one of the following which is the BEST reason why this is important is that it may

    A. help you to set up good communications between you and your workers
    B. give you a better understanding of the purpose of the project
    C. give you control over the time and cost involved in the project
    D. help you to determine who are your most productive workers

    11._____

12. When doing work planning for your shop, the factor that you should normally consider LAST among the following is knowing your

    A. major objectives
    B. record keeping system
    C. minor objectives
    D. priorities

13. You have the responsibility for ordering all materials for your maintenance shop. A listing of materials needed for the operations of your shop is long overdue. You realize that you are unable to find time to take care of the inventory personally because of a high priority project you have been working on which has been taking all of your time. You do not know when you will be finished with the project.
    The BEST of the following courses of action to take in handling this inventory matter is to

    A. request that you be taken off the project immediately so that you may take care of the inventory
    B. complete your high priority project and then do the inventory yourself
    C. volunteer to work overtime so that you may complete the inventory while continuing with the project
    D. assign the inventory work to a competent subordinate

14. You have the authority and responsibility for seeing that proper records are kept in your shop. Assume that you decide to delegate to a records clerk the responsibility for collecting the time sheets and the authority to make changes on the time sheets to correct the information when necessary.
    Of the following, which one is the BEST argument that can be made regarding your decision?

    A. *Unacceptable*; because you can delegate only your responsibility but none of your authority to the records clerk
    B. *Acceptable*; because you can delegate some of your authority and some of your responsibility to the records clerk
    C. *Unacceptable;* because you can delegate only your authority but none of your responsibility to the records clerk
    D. *Acceptable;* because you can delegate all your responsibility and all your authority to the records clerk

15. You will LEAST likely be able to do an effective job of controlling operating costs if you

    A. eliminate idle time
    B. reduce absenteeism
    C. raise your budget
    D. combine work operations

16. Of the following actions, the one which is LEAST likely to help in carrying out your responsibilities of looking after the interests of your workers is to

    A. crack down on your workers when necessary
    B. let your workers know that you support company policy
    C. prevent the transfers of your workers
    D. back up your workers in a controversy

17. The term *accountability*, as used in management of supervision, means MOST NEARLY

    A. responsibility for results
    B. record keeping
    C. bookkeeping systems
    D. inventory control

18. Assume that you have been unable to convince an employee of the seriousness of his poor attendance record by talking to him.
The one of the following which is the BEST course of action for you to take is to

    A. keep talking to the employee
    B. recommend that a written warning be given
    C. consider transferring the employee to another work location
    D. recommend that the employee be fired

19. When delegating work to a subordinate foreman, you should NOT

    A. delegate the right to make any decisions
    B. be interested in the results of the work, but in the method of doing the work
    C. delegate any work that you can do better than your subordinate
    D. give up your final responsibility for the work

20. Of the following statements, the BEST reason why proper scheduling of maintenance work is important is that it

    A. eliminates the need for individual job work orders
    B. classifies job skills in accordance with performance
    C. minimizes lost time in performing any maintenance job
    D. determines needed repairs in various locations

21. Of the following factors, the one which is of LEAST importance in determining the number of subordinates that an individual should be assigned to supervise is the

    A. nature of the work being supervised
    B. qualifications of the individual as a supervisor
    C. capabilities of the subordinates
    D. lines of promotion for the subordinates

22. Suppose that a large number of semi-literate residents of this city have been requesting the assistance of your department. You are asked to prepare a form which these applicants will be required to fill out before their requests will be considered.
In view of these facts, the one of the following factors to which you should give the GREATEST amount of consideration in preparing this form is the

    A. size of the form
    B. sequence of the information asked for on the form
    C. level of difficulty of the language used in the form
    D. number of times which the form will have to be reviewed

23. A budget is a plan whereby a goal is set for future operations. It affords a medium for comparing actual expenditures with planned expenditures.
The one of the following which is the MOST accurate statement on the basis of this statement is that

    A. the budget serves as an accurate measure of past as well as future expenditures
    B. the budget presents an estimate of expenditures to be made in the future
    C. budget estimates should be based upon past budget requirements
    D. planned expenditures usually fall short of actual expenditures

24. A foreman who is familiar with modern management principles should know that the one of the following requirements of an administrator which is LEAST important is his ability to

    A. coordinate work
    B. plan, organize, and direct the work under his control
    C. cooperate with others
    D. perform the duties of the employees under his jurisdiction

25. The one of the following which should be considered the LEAST important objective of the service rating system is to

    A. rate the employees on the basis of their potential abilities
    B. establish a basis for assigning employees to special types of work
    C. provide a means of recognizing superior work performance
    D. reveal the need for training as well as the effectiveness of a training program

KEY (CORRECT ANSWERS)

1. A		11. C	
2. A		12. B	
3. B		13. D	
4. C		14. B	
5. B		15. C	
6. A		16. C	
7. D		17. A	
8. A		18. B	
9. D		19. D	
10. D		20. C	

21. D
22. C
23. B
24. D
25. A

SUPERVISION, ADMINISTRATION, MANAGEMENT AND ORGANIZATION
EXAMINATION SECTION

TEST 1

DIRECTIONS: Each question or incomplete statement is followed by several suggested answers or completions. Select the one that BEST answers the question or completes the statement. *PRINT THE LETTER OF THE CORRECT ANSWER IN THE SPACE AT THE RIGHT.*

1. The one of the following practices by a supervisor which is MOST likely to lead to confusion and inefficiency is for him to
    A. give orders verbally directly to the man assigned to the job
    B. issue orders only in writing
    C. follow up his orders after issuing them
    D. relay his orders to the men through co-workers

2. If you are given an oral order by a supervisor which you do not understand completely, you should
    A. use your own judgment
    B. discuss the order with your men
    C. ask your supervisor for a further explanation
    D. carry out that part of the order which you do understand and then ask for more information

3. An orientation program for a group of new employees should NOT ordinarily include a
    A. review of the organizational structure of the agency
    B. detailed description of the duties of each new employee
    C. description of the physical layout of the repair shop
    D. statement of the rules pertaining to sick leave, vacation, and holidays

4. The MOST important rule to follow with regard to discipline is that a man should be disciplined
    A. after everyone has had time to "cool off"
    B. as soon as possible after the infraction of rules
    C. only for serious rule violations
    D. before he makes a mistake

5. If the men under your supervision continue to work effectively even when you are out sick for several days, it would MOST probably indicate that
    A. the men are merely trying to show you up
    B. the men are in constant fear of you and are glad you are away
    C. you have trained your men properly and have their full cooperation
    D. you are serving no useful purpose since the men can get along without you

6. When evaluating subordinates, the employee who should be rated HIGHEST by his supervisor is the one who
   A. never lets the supervisor do heavy lifting
   B. asks many questions about the work
   C. makes many suggestions on work procedures
   D. listens to instructions and carries them out

7. Of the following, the factor which is generally MOST important to the conduct of successful training is
   A. time   B. preparation   C. equipment   D. space

8. One of the MAJOR disadvantages of "on-the-job" training is that it
   A. requires a long training period for instructors
   B. may not be progressive
   C. requires additional equipment
   D. may result in the waste of supplies

9. For a supervisor to train workers in several trades which involve various skills, presents many training problems.
   The one of the following which is NOT true in such a training situation is that
   A. less supervision is required
   B. greater planning for training is required
   C. rotation of assignments is necessary
   D. less productivity can be expected

10. For a supervisor of repair workers to have each worker specialize in learning a single trade is GENERALLY
    A. *desirable*; each worker will become expert in his assigned trade
    B. *undesirable*; there is less flexibility of assignments possible when each worker has learned only a single trade
    C. *desirable*; the training responsibility of the supervisor is simplified when each worker is required to learn a single trade
    D. *undesirable*; workers lose interest quickly when they know they are expected to learn a single trade

11. An IMPORTANT advantage of standardizing work procedures is that it
    A. develops all-around skills
    B. makes the work less monotonous
    C. provides an incentive for good work
    D. enable the work to be done with less supervision

12. Generally, the GREATEST difficulty in introducing new work methods is due to the fact that
    A. men become set in their ways
    B. the old way is generally better
    C. only the department will benefit from changes
    D. explaining new methods is time consuming

13. Assume that you are required to transmit an order with, which you do not agree, to your subordinates.
    In this case, it would be BEST for you to
    A. ask one of your superiors to transmit the order
    B. refuse to transmit an order with which you do not agree
    C. transmit the order but be sure to explain that you do not agree with it
    D. transmit the order and enforce it to the best of your ability

14. The MAIN reason for written orders is that
    A. proper blame can be placed if the order is not carried out
    B. the order will be carried out faster
    C. the order can be properly analyzed as to its meaning
    D. there will be no doubt as to what the order says

15. You have been informed unofficially by another shop manager that some of the men under your supervision are loafing on the job.
    This situation can be BEST handled by
    A. telling the man to mind his own business
    B. calling the men together and reprimanding them
    C. having the men work under your direct supervision
    D. arranging to make spot checks at more frequent intervals

16. Suggestions on improving methods of doing work, when submitted by a new employee, should be
    A. examined for possible merit because the new man may have a fresh viewpoint
    B. ignored because it would make the old employees resentful
    C. disregarded because he is too unfamiliar with the work
    D. examined only for the purpose of judging the new man

17. One of your employees often slows down the work of his crew by playing practical jokes.
    The BEST way to handle this situation is to
    A. arrange for his assignment to more than his share of unpleasant jobs
    B. warn him that he must stop this practice at once
    C. ignore this situation for he will soon tire of it
    D. ask your supervisor to transfer him

18. One of your men is always complaining about working conditions, equipment, and his fellow workers.
    The BEST action for you to take in this situation is to
    A. have this man work alone if possible
    B. consider each complaint on is merits
    C. tell him bluntly that you will not listen to any of his complaints
    D. give this man the worst jobs until he quits complaining

19. It is generally agreed that men who are interested in their work will do the best work.
    A supervisor can LEAST stimulate this interest by
    A. complimenting men on good work
    B. correcting men on their working procedures
    C. striving to create overtime for his men
    D. recommending merit raises for excellent work

20. If you, as a supervisor, have criticized one of your men for making a mistake, you should
    A. remind the man of his error from time to time to keep him on his toes
    B. overlook any further errors which this man may make, otherwise he may feel he is a victim of discrimination
    C. give the man the opportunity to redeem himself
    D. impress the man with the fact that all his work will be closely checked from then on

21. In his efforts to maintain standards of performance, a shop manager uses a system of close supervision to detect or catch errors.
    An *opposite* method of accomplishing the *same* objective is to employ a program which
    A. instills in each employee a pride of workmanship to do the job correctly the first time
    B. groups each job accordingly to the importance to the overall objectives of the program
    C. makes the control of quality the responsibility of an inspector
    D. emphasizes that there is a "one" best way for an employee to do s specific job

22. Assume that after taking over a repair shop, a shop manager feels that he is taking too much time maintaining records.
    He should
    A. temporarily assign this job to one of his senior repair crew chiefs
    B. get together with his supervisor to determine if all these records are needed
    C. stop keeping those records which he believes are unnecessary
    D. spend a few additional hours each day until his records are current

23. In order to apply performance standards to employees engaged in repair shop activities, a shop manager must FIRST
    A. allow workers to decide for themselves the way to do the job
    B. determine what is acceptable as satisfactory work
    C. separate the more difficult tasks from the simpler tasks
    D. stick to an established work schedule

24. Of the following actions a shop manager can take to determine whether the vehicles used in his shop are being utilized properly, the one which will give him the LEAST meaningful information is
    A. conducting an analysis of vehicle assignments
    B. reviewing the number of miles traveled by each vehicle with and without loads
    C. recording the unloaded weights of each vehicle
    D. comparing the amount of time vehicles are parked at job sites with the time required to travel to and from job sites

24.____

25. For a shop manager, the MOST important reason that equipment which is used infrequently should be considered for disposal is that
    A. the time required for its maintenance could be better used elsewhere
    B. such equipment may cause higher management to think that your shop is not busy
    C. the men may resent having to work on such equipment
    D. such equipment usually has a higher breakdown rate in operation

25.____

KEY (CORRECT ANSWERS)

1.	D		11.	D
2.	C		12.	A
3.	B		13.	D
4.	B		14.	D
5.	C		15.	D
6.	D		16.	A
7.	B		17.	B
8.	B		18.	B
9.	A		19.	C
10.	B		20.	C

21.	A
22.	B
23.	B
24.	C
25.	A

TEST 2

DIRECTIONS: Each question or incomplete statement is followed by several suggested answers or completions. Select the one that BEST answers the question or completes the statement. *PRINT THE LETTER OF THE CORRECT ANSWER IN THE SPACE AT THE RIGHT.*

1. Assume that one of your subordinates approaches you with a grievance concerning working conditions.
   Of the following, the BEST action for you to take first is to
   A. "soft-soap" him, since most grievances are imaginary
   B. settle the grievance to his satisfaction
   C. try to talk him out of his complaint
   D. listen patiently and sincerely to the complaint

   1.____

2. Of the following, the BEST way for a supervisor to help a subordinate learn a new skill which requires the use of tools is for him to give this subordinate
   A. a list of good books on the subject
   B. lectures on the theoretical aspects of the task
   C. opportunities to watch someone using the tools
   D. opportunities to practice the skill, under close supervision

   2.____

3. A supervisor finds that his own work load is excessive because several of his subordinates are unable to complete their assignments.
   Of the following, the BEST action for him to take to improve this situation is to
   A. discipline these subordinates
   B. work overtime
   C. request additional staff
   D. train these subordinates in more efficient work methods

   3.____

4. The one of the following situations which is MOST likely to be the result of *poor* morale is a(n)
   A. high rate of turnover
   B. decrease in number of requests by subordinates for transfers
   C. increase in the backlog of work
   D. decrease in the rate of absenteeism

   4.____

5. As a supervisor, you find that several of your subordinates are not meeting their deadlines because they are doing work assigned to them by one of your fellow supervisors without your knowledge.
   Of the following, the BEST course of action for you to take in this situation is to
   A. tell the other supervisors to make future assignments through you
   B. assert your authority by publicly telling the other supervisors to stop issuing orders to your workers
   C. go along with this practice; it is an effective way to fully utilize the available manpower
   D. take the matter directly to your immediate supervisor without delay

   5.____

6. If a supervisor of a duplicating section in an agency hears a rumor concerning a change in agency personnel policy through the "grapevine," he should
   A. *repeat* it to his subordinates so they will be informed
   B. *not repeat* it to his subordinates before he determines the facts because, as supervisor, his work may give it unwarranted authority
   C. *repeat* it to his subordinates so that they will like him for confiding in them
   D. *not repeat* it to his subordinates before he determines the facts because a duplicating section is not concerned with matters of policy

6.____

7. When teaching a new employee how to operate a machine, a supervisor should FIRST
   A. let the employee try to operate the machine by himself, since he can learn only by his mistakes
   B. explain the process to him with the use of diagrams before showing him the machine
   C. have him memorize the details of the operation from the manual
   D. explain and demonstrate the various steps in the process, making sure he understands each step

7.____

8. If a subordinate accuses you of always giving him the least desirable assignments, you should IMMEDIATELY
   A. tell him that it is not true and you do not want to hear any more about it
   B. try to get specific details from him, so that you can find out what his impressions are based on
   C. tell him that you distribute assignments in the fairest way possible and he must be mistaken
   D. ask him what current assignment he has that he does not like, and assign it to someone else

8.____

9. Suppose that the production of an operator under your supervision has been unsatisfactory and you have decided to have a talk with him about it.
During the interview, it would be BEST for you to
   A. discuss only the subordinate's weak points so that he can overcome them
   B. discuss only the subordinate's strong points so that he will not become discouraged
   C. compare the subordinate's work with that of his co-workers so that he will know what is expected of him
   D. discuss both his weak and strong points so that he will get a view of his overall performance

9.____

10. Suppose that an operator under your supervision makes a mistake in color on a 2,000-page job and runs it on white paper instead of on blue paper.
Of the following, your BEST course in these circumstances would be to point out the error to the operator and
   A. have the operator rerun the job immediately on blue paper
   B. send the job to the person who ordered it without comment
   C. send the job to the person who ordered it and tell him it could not be done on blue paper
   D. ask the person who ordered the job whether the white paper is acceptable

10.____

11. Assuming that all your subordinates have equal technical competence, the BEST policy for a supervisor to follow when making assignments of undesirable jobs would be to
    A. distribute them as evenly as possible among his subordinates
    B. give them to the subordinate with the poorest attendance record
    C. ask the subordinate with the least seniority to do them
    D. assign them to the subordinate who is least likely to complain

11.____

12. To get the BEST results when training a number of subordinates at the same time, a supervisor should
    A. treat all of them in an identical manner to avoid accusations of favoritism
    B. treat them all fairly, but use different approaches in dealing with people of different personality types
    C. train only one subordinate, and have him train the others, because this will save a lot of the supervisor's time
    D. train first the subordinates who learn quickly so as to make the others think that the operation is easy to learn

12.____

13. Assume that, after a week's vacation, you return to find that one of your subordinates has produced a job which is unsatisfactory.
    Your BEST course of action at that time would be to
    A. talk to your personnel department about implementing disciplinary action
    B. discuss unsatisfactory work in the unit at a meeting with all of your subordinates
    C. discuss the job with the subordinate to determine why he was unable to do it properly
    D. ignore the matter, because it is too late to correct the mistake

13.____

14. Suppose that an operator under your supervision informs you that Mr. Y, a senior administrator in your agency, has been submitting for copying many papers which are obviously personal in nature. The operator wants to know what to do about it, since the duplication of personal papers is against agency rules.
    Your BEST course of action in these circumstances would be to
    A. tell the operator to pretend not to notice the content of the material and continue to copy whatever is given to him
    B. tell the operator that Mr. Y, as a senior administrator, must have gotten special permission to have personal papers duplicated
    C. have the operator refer Mr. Y to you and inform Mr. Y yourself that duplication of personal papers is against agency rules
    D. call Mr. Y's superior and tell him that Mr. Y has been having personal papers duplicated, which is against agency rules

14.____

15. Assume that you are teaching a certain process to an operator under your supervision.
    In order to BEST determine whether he is actually learning what you are teaching, you should ask questions which
    A. can easily be answered by a "yes" or "no"
    B. require or encourage guessing

15.____

C. require a short description of what has been taught
D. are somewhat ambiguous so as to make the learner think about the procedures in question

16. If an employee is chronically late or absent, as his supervisor, it would be BEST for you to
    A. let his work pile up so he can see that no one else will do it for him
    B. discuss the matter with him and stress the importance of finding a solution
    C. threaten to enter a written report on the matter into his personnel file
    D. work out a system with him so he can have a different work schedule than the other employees

17. Assume that you have a subordinate who has just finished a basic training course in the operation of a machine.
    Giving him a large and difficult FIRST assignment would be
    A. *good*, because it would force him to "learn the ropes"
    B. *bad*, because he would probably have difficulty in carrying it out, discouraging him and resulting in a waste of time and supplies
    C. *good*, because how he handles it would give you an excellent basis for judging his competence
    D. *bad*, because he would probably assume that you are discriminating against him

18. After putting a new employee under your supervision through an initial training period, assigning him to work with a more experienced employee for a while would be a
    A. *good* idea, because it would give him the opportunity to observe what he had been taught and to participate in production himself
    B. *bad* idea, because he should not be required to work under the direction of anyone who is not his supervisor
    C. *good* idea, because it would raise the morale of the more experienced employee who could use him to do all the unpleasant chores
    D. *bad* idea, because the best way for him to learn would be to give him full responsibility for assignments right away

19. Assume that a supervisor is responsible for ordering supplies for the duplicating section in his agency.
    Which one of the following actions would be MOST helpful in determining when to place orders so that an adequate supply of materials will be on hand at all times?
    A. Taking an inventory of supplies on hand at least every two months
    B. Asking his subordinates to inform him when they see that supplies are low
    C. Checking the inventory of supplies whenever he has time
    D. Keeping a running inventory of supplies and a record of estimated needs

20. Routine procedures that have worked well in the past should be reviewed periodically by a supervisor MAINLY because
    A. they may have become outdated or in need of revision
    B. employees might dislike the procedures even though they have proven successful in the past
    C. these reviews are the main part of a supervisor's job
    D. this practice serves to give the supervisor an idea of how productive his subordinates are

21. Assume that an employee tells his supervisor about a grievance he has against a co-worker. The supervisor assures the employee that he will immediately take action to eliminate the grievance.
    The supervisor's attitude should be considered
    A. *correct*, because a good supervisor is one who can come to a quick decision
    B. *incorrect*, because the supervisor should have told the employee that he will investigate the grievance and then determine a future course of action
    C. *correct*, because the employee's morale will be higher, resulting in greater productivity
    D. *incorrect*, because the supervisor should remain uninvolved and let the employees settle grievances between themselves

22. If an employee's work output is low and of poor quality due to faulty work habits, the MOST constructive of the following ways for a supervisor to correct this situation generally is to
    A. discipline the employee
    B. transfer the employee to another unit
    C. provide additional training
    D. check the employee's work continuously

23. Assume that it becomes necessary for a supervisor to ask his staff to work overtime.
    Which one of the following techniques is MOST likely to win their willing cooperation to do this?
    A. Explain that this is part of their job specification entitled, "performs related work"
    B. Explain the reason it is necessary for the employees to work overtime
    C. Promise the employees special consideration regarding future leave matters
    D. Explain that if the employees do not work overtime, they will face possible disciplinary action

24. If an employee's work performance has recently fallen below established minimum standards for quality and quantity, the threat of demotion or other disciplinary measures as an attempt to improve this employee's performance would probably be the MOST acceptable and effective course of action
    A. *only* after other more constructive measures have failed
    B. *if* applied uniformly to all employees as soon as performance falls below standard

25. If, as a supervisor, it becomes necessary for you to assign an employee to supervise your unit during your vacation, it would generally be BEST to select the employee who
    A. is the best technician on the staff
    B. can get the work out smoothly, without friction
    C. has the most seniority
    D. is the most popular with the group

25.____

KEY (CORRECT ANSWERS)

1.	D		11.	A
2.	D		12.	B
3.	D		13.	C
4.	A		14.	C
5.	A		15.	C
6.	B		16.	B
7.	D		17.	B
8.	B		18.	A
9.	D		19.	D
10.	D		20.	A

21. B
22. C
23. B
24. A
25. B

TEST 3

DIRECTIONS: Each question or incomplete statement is followed by several suggested answers or completions. Select the one that BEST answers the question or completes the statement. *PRINT THE LETTER OF THE CORRECT ANSWER IN THE SPACE AT THE RIGHT.*

1. An employee under your supervision has demonstrated a deep-seated personality problem that has begun to affect his work.
   This situation should be
   A. *ignored*, mainly because such problems usually resolve themselves
   B. *handled*, mainly because the employee should be assisted in seeking professional help
   C. *ignored*, mainly because the employee will consider any advice as interference
   D. *handled*, mainly because the supervisors should be qualified to resolve deep-seated personality problems

   1.____

2. Of the following, a supervisor will usually be MOST successful in maintaining employee morale while providing effective leadership if he
   A. takes prompt disciplinary action every time it is needed
   B. gives difficult assignments only to those workers who ask for such work
   C. promises his workers anything reasonable they request
   D. relies entirely on his staff for decisions

   2.____

3. When a supervisor makes an assignment to his subordinates, he should include a clear statement of what results are expected when the assignment is completed.
   Of the following, the BEST reason for following this procedure is that it will
   A. make it unnecessary for the supervisor to check on the progress of the work
   B. stimulate initiative and cooperation on the part of the more responsible workers
   C. give the subordinates a way to judge whether their work is meeting the requirements
   D. give the subordinates the feeling that they have some freedom of action

   3.____

4. Assume that, on a new employee's first day of work, his supervisor gives him a good orientation by telling him the general regulations and procedures used in the office and introducing him to his department head and fellow employees.
   For the remainder of the day, it would be BEST for the supervisor to
   A. give him steady instruction in all phases of his job, while stressing its most important aspects
   B. have him observe a fellow employee perform the duties of the job
   C. instruct him in that part of the job which he would prefer to learn first
   D. give him a simple task which requires little instruction and allows him to familiarize himself with the surroundings

   4.____

5. When it becomes necessary to criticize subordinates because several errors in the unit's work have been discovered, the supervisor should USUALLY
    A. focus on the job operation and avoid placing personal blame
    B. make every effort to fix blame and admonish the person responsible
    C. include in the criticism those employees who recognize and rectify their own mistakes
    D. repeat the criticism at regular intervals in order to impress the subordinates with the seriousness of their errors

6. If two employees under your supervision are continually bickering and cannot get along together, the FIRST action that you should take is to
    A. investigate possible ways of separating them
    B. ask your immediate superior for the procedure to follow in this situation
    C. determine the cause of their difficulty
    D. develop a plan and tell both parties to try it

7. In general, it is appropriate to recommend the transfer of an employee for all of the following reasons EXCEPT
    A. rewarding him
    B. providing him with a more challenging job
    C. remedying an error in initial placement
    D. disciplining him

8. Of the following, the MAIN disadvantage of basing a training and development program on a series of lectures is that the lecture technique
    A. does not sufficiently involve trainees in the learning process
    B. is more costly than other methods of training
    C. cannot be used to facilitate the understanding of difficult information
    D. is time consuming and inefficient

9. A supervisor has been assigned to train a new employee who is properly motivated but has made many mistakes.
    In the interview between the supervisor and employee about this problem, the employee should FIRST be
    A. asked if he can think of anything that he can do to improve his work
    B. complimented sincerely on some aspect of his work that is satisfactory
    C. asked to explain why he made the mistake
    D. advised that he may be dismissed if he continues to be careless

10. In training subordinates for more complex work, a supervisor must be aware of the progress that the subordinates are making.
    Determination of the results that have been accomplished by training is a concept commonly known as
    A. reinforcement
    B. feedback
    C. cognitive dissonance
    D. the halo effect

11. Assume that one of your subordinates loses interest in his work because he feels that your recent evaluation of his performance was unfair.
    The one of the following which is the BEST way to help him is to
    A. establish frequent deadlines for his work
    B. discuss his feelings and attitude with him
    C. discuss with him only the positive aspects of his performance
    D. arrange for his transfer to another unit

12. Informal organizations often develop at work.
    Of the following, the supervisor should realize that these groups will USUALLY
    A. determine work pace through unofficial agreements
    B. restrict vital communication channels
    C. lower morale by providing a chance to spread grievances
    D. provide leaders who will substitute for the supervisor when he is absent

13. Assume that you, the supervisor, have called to your office a subordinate whom, on several recent occasions, you have seen using the office telephone for personal use.
    In this situation, it would be MOST appropriate to begin the interview by
    A. discussing the disciplinary action that you believe to be warranted
    B. asking the subordinate to explain the reason for his personal use of the office telephone
    C. telling the subordinate about other employees who were disciplined for the same offense
    D. informing the subordinate that he is not to use the office telephone under any circumstances until further notice

14. Of the following, the success of any formal training program depends PRIMARILY upon the
    A. efficient and thorough preparation of materials, facilities, and procedures for instruction
    B. training program's practical relevance to the on-the-job situation
    C. scheduling of training sessions so as to minimize interference with normal job responsibilities
    D. creation of a positive initial reception on the part of the trainees

15. All of the following are legitimate purposes for regularly evaluating employee performance EXCEPT
    A. stimulating improvement in performance
    B. developing more accurate standards to be used in future ratings
    C. encouraging a spirit of competition
    D. allowing the employee to set realistic work goals for himself

16. A certain supervisor is very conscientious. He wants to receive personally all reports, correspondence, etc., and to be completely involved in all of the unit's operations. However, he is having difficulty in keeping up with the growing amount of paperwork.

Of the following, the MOST desirable course of action for him to take is to
- A. put in more hours on the job
- B. ask for additional office help
- C. begin to delegate more of his work
- D. inquire of his supervisor if the paperwork is really necessary

17. Assume that you are a supervisor. One of the workers under your supervision expresses his need to speak to you about a client who has been particularly uncooperative in providing information.
The MOST appropriate action for you to take FIRST would be to
    - A. agree to see the client for the worker in order to get the information
    - B. advise the worker to try several more times to get the information before he asks you for help
    - C. tell the worker you will go with him to see the client in order to observe his technique
    - D. ask the worker some questions in order to determine the type of help he needs in the situation

18. The supervisor who is MOST likely to achieve a high level of productivity from the professional employees under his supervision is the one who
    - A. watches their progress continuously
    - B. provides them with just enough information to carry out their assigned tasks
    - C. occasionally pitches in and helps them with their work
    - D. shares with them responsibility for setting work goals

19. Assume that there has been considerable friction for some time among the workers of a certain unit. The supervisor in charge of this unit becomes aware that the problem is getting serious as shown by increased absenteeism and lateness, loud arguments, etc.
Of the following, the BEST course of action for the supervisor to take FIRST is to
    - A. have a staff discussion about objectives and problems
    - B. seek out and penalize the apparent trouble-makers
    - C. set up and enforce stricter formal rules
    - D. discipline the next subordinate who causes friction

20. Assume that an employee under your supervision asks you for some blank paper and pencils to take home to her young grandson who, she says, delights in drawing.
The one of the following actions you SHOULD take is to
    - A. give her the material she wants and refrain from any comment
    - B. refuse her request and tell her that the use of office supplies for personal reasons is not proper
    - C. give her the material but suggest that she buy it next time
    - D. tell her to take the material herself since you do not want to know anything about the matter

21. A certain supervisor is given a performance evaluation by his superior. In it he is commended for his method of "delegation," a term that USUALLY refers to the action of
    A. determining the priorities for activities which must be completed
    B. assigning to subordinates some of the duties for which he is responsible
    C. standardizing operations in order to achieve results as close as possible to established goals
    D. dividing the activities necessary to achieve an objective into simple steps

22. A supervisor is approached by a subordinate who complains that a fellow worker is not assuming his share of the workload and is, therefore, causing more work for others in the office.
    Of the following, the MOST appropriate action for the supervisor to take in response to this complaint is to tell the subordinate
    A. that he will look into the matter
    B. to concentrate on his own job and not to worry about others
    C. to discuss the matter with the other worker
    D. that not everyone is capable of working at the same pace

23. Aside from the formal relationships established by management, informal and unofficial relationships will be developed among the personnel within an organization.
    Of the following, the MAIN importance of such informal relationships to the operations of the formal organization is that they
    A. reinforce the basic goals of the formal organization
    B. insure the interchangeability of the personnel within the organization
    C. provide an additional channel of communications within the organization
    D. insure predictability and control of the behavior of members of the organization

24. The most productive worker in a unit frequently takes overly-long coffee breaks and lunch hours while maintaining his above-average rate of productivity.
    Of the following, it would be MOST advisable for the supervisor to
    A. reprimand him, because rules must be enforced equally regardless of the merit of an individual's job performance
    B. ignore the infractions because a superior worker should be granted extra privileges for his efforts
    C. take no action unless others in the unit complain, because a reprimand may hurt the superior worker's feelings and cause him to produce less
    D. tell other members of the unit that a comparable rate of productivity on their part will be rewarded with similar privileges

25. A supervisor has been asked by his superior to choose an employee to supervise a special project.
    Of the following, the MOST significant factor to consider in making this choice is the employee's
    A. length of service
    B. ability to do the job
    C. commitment to the goals of the agency
    D. attitude toward his fellow workers

25.____

KEY (CORRECT ANSWERS)

1.	B		11.	B
2.	A		12.	A
3.	C		13.	B
4.	D		14.	B
5.	A		15.	C
6.	C		16.	C
7.	D		17.	D
8.	A		18.	D
9.	B		19.	A
10.	B		20.	B

21.	B
22.	A
23.	C
24.	A
25.	B

TEST 4

DIRECTIONS: Each question or incomplete statement is followed by several suggested answers or completions. Select the one that BEST answers the question or completes the statement. *PRINT THE LETTER OF THE CORRECT ANSWER IN THE SPACE AT THE RIGHT.*

1. Assume that you are a newly appointed supervisor. 1.____
Your MOST important responsibility is to
    A. make certain that all of the employees under your supervision are treated equally
    B. reduce disciplinary situations to a minimum
    C. insure an atmosphere of mutual trust between your workers and yourself
    D. see that the required work is done properly

2. In order to make sure that work is completed on time, the supervisor should 2.____
    A. pitch in and do as much of the work herself as she can
    B. schedule the work and control its progress
    C. not assign more than one person to any one task
    D. assign the same amount of work to each subordinate

3. Assume that you are a supervisor in charge of a number of workers who do the same kind of work and who each produce about the same volume of work in a given period of time. 3.____
When their performance is evaluated, the worker who should be rated as the MOST accurate is the one
    A. whose errors are the easiest to correct
    B. whose errors involve the smallest amount of money
    C. who makes the fewest errors in her work
    D. who makes fewer errors as she becomes more experienced

4. As a supervisor, you have been asked by the manager to recommend whether the work of the bookkeeping office requires a permanent increase in bookkeeping office staff. 4.____
Of the following questions, the one whose answer would be MOST likely to assist you in making your recommendation is:
    A. Are temporary employees hired to handle seasonal fluctuations in work loads?
    B. Are some permanent employees working irregular hours because they occasionally work overtime?
    C. Are the present permanent employees keeping the work of the bookkeeping office current?
    D. Are employees complaining that the work is unevenly divided?

2 (#4)

5. Assume that you are a supervisor. One of your subordinates tells you that he is dissatisfied with his work assignment and that he wishes to discuss the matter with you. The employee is obviously very angry and upset.
Of the following, the course of action that you should take FIRST in this situation is to
   A. promise the employee that you will review all the work assignments in the office to determine whether any changes should be made.
   B. have the employee present his complaint, correcting him whenever he makes what seems to be an erroneous charge against you
   C. postpone discussion of the employee's complaint, explaining to him that the matter can be settled more satisfactory if it is discussed calmly
   D. permit the employee to present his complaint in full, withholding your comments until he has finished making his complaint

5.____

6. Assume that you are a supervisor. You find that you are spending too much time on routine tasks and not enough time on supervision of the work of your subordinates.
It would be ADVISABLE for you to
   A. assign some of the routine tasks to your subordinates
   B. postpone the performance of routine tasks until you have completed your supervisory tasks
   C. delegate the supervisory work to a capable subordinate
   D. eliminate some of the supervisory tasks that you are required to perform

6.____

7. Assume that you are a supervisor. You discover that one of your workers has violated an important rule.
The FIRST course of action for you as the supervisor to take would be to
   A. call a meeting of the entire staff and discuss the matter generally without mentioning any employee by name
   B. arrange to supervise the offending worker's activities more closely
   C. discuss the violation privately with the worker involved
   D. discuss the matter with the worker within hearing of the entire staff so that she will feel too ashamed to commit this violation in the future

7.____

8. As a supervisor, you are to prepare a vacation schedule for the bookkeeping office employees.
The one of the following that is the LEAST important factor for you to consider in setting up this schedule is
   A. seniority   B. vacation preferences of employees
   C. average productivity of the office

8.____

9. In assigning a complicated task to a group of subordinates, a certain supervisor does not indicate the specific steps to be followed in performing the assignment, nor does he designate which subordinate is to be responsible for seeing that the task is done on time.

9.____

This supervisor's method of assigning the task is MOST likely to result in
- A. confusion among subordinates with consequent delays in work
- B. greater individual effort and self-reliance
- C. assumption of authority by capable subordinates
- D. loss of confidence by subordinates in their ability

10. While you are explaining a new procedure to an employee, she asks you a question about the procedure which you cannot answer.
The MOST appropriate action for you to take is to
    - A. admit your inability to answer the question and promise to obtain the information
    - B. point out the likelihood of a situation arising which would require an answer to the question
    - C. ask the worker to give her reason for asking the question before you give any further reply
    - D. tell her to inform you immediately should a situation arise requiring an answer to her question

KEY (CORRECT ANSWERS)

1.	D	6.	A
2.	B	7.	C
3.	C	8.	C
4.	C	9.	A
5.	D	10.	A

EXAMINATION SECTION
TEST 1

DIRECTIONS: Each question or incomplete statement is followed by several suggested answers or completions. Select the one that BEST answers the question or completes the statement. *PRINT THE LETTER OF THE CORRECT ANSWER IN THE SPACE AT THE RIGHT.*

1. At times there may be a conflict between employees' needs and agency goals. A supervisor's MAIN role in motivating employees in such circumstances is to try to
    A. develop good work habits among the employees whom he supervises
    B. emphasize the importance of material rewards such as merit increases
    C. keep careful records of employees' performance for possible disciplinary action
    D. reconcile employees' objectives with those of the public agency

1.____

2. Organizations cannot function effectively without policies.
However, when an organization imposes excessively detailed policy restrictions, it is MOST likely to lead to
    A. conflicts among individual employees
    B. a lack of adequate supervision
    C. a reduction of employee initiative
    D. a reliance on punitive discipline

2.____

3. The PRIMARY responsibility for establishing good employee relations in the public service usually rests with
    A. employees
    B. management
    C. civil service organizations
    D. employee organizations

3.____

4. At times, certain off-the-job conduct of public employees may be of concern to management. This concern stems from the fact that
    A. agency programs could be harmed by adverse publicity if employees' conduct is considered detrimental by the public
    B. fairness to all concerned is usually the major consideration in disciplinary cases
    C. public employees must meet higher standards than employees working in private industry
    D. public employees have high ethical standards and may participate in social action programs

4.____

5. At one time or another, most employees ask for, or expect, special treatment. For a supervisor faced with this problem, the one of the following which is the MOST valid guideline is:
    A. According to the rules, a supervisor must give identical treatment to all his subordinates, regardless of the circumstances.

5.____

B. Although all employees have equal rights, it is sometimes necessary to give an employee special treatment to meet an individual need.
C. It would damage morale if any employee were to receive special treatment, regardless of circumstances.
D. Since each employee has different needs, there is little reason to maintain general rules.

6. Mental health problems exist in many parts of our society and may also be found in the work setting.
The BASIC role of the supervisor in relation to the mental health problems of his subordinates is to
   A. restrict himself solely to the taking of disciplinary measures, if warranted, and follow up carefully
   B. avoid involvement in personal matters
   C. identify mental health problems as early as possible
   D. resolve mental health problems through personal counseling

6.____

7. Supervisory expectation of high levels of employee performance, where such performance is possible, is MOST likely to lead to employees'
   A. expecting frequent praise and encouragement
   B. gaining a greater sense of satisfaction
   C. needing less detailed instructions than previously
   D. reducing their quantitative output

7.____

8. In public agencies, as elsewhere, supervisors sometimes compete with one another to increase their units' productivity.
Of the following, the MAJOR disadvantage of such competition, from the general viewpoint of providing good public service, is that
   A. while individual employee effort will increase, unit productivity will decrease
   B. employees will be discouraged from sincere interest in their work
   C. the supervisors' competition may hinder the achievement of agency goals
   D. total payroll costs will increase as the activities of each unit increase

8.____

9. If employees are motivated primarily by material compensation, the amount of effort an individual employee will put into performing his work effectively will depend MAINLY upon how he perceives
   A. cooperation to be tied to successful effort
   B. the association between good work and increased compensation
   C. the public status of his particular position
   D. the supervisor's behavior in work situations

9.____

10. Cash awards to individual employees are sometimes used to encourage useful suggestions. However, some management experts believe that awards should involve some form of employee recognition other than cash.
Which of the following reasons BEST supports opposition to using cash as a reward for worthwhile suggestions?

10.____

A. Cash awards cause employees to expend excessive time in making suggestions.
B. Taxpayer opposition to dash awards has increased following generous salary increases for public employees in recent years.
C. Public funds expended on awards leads to a poor image of public employees.
D. The use of cash awards raises the problem of deciding the monetary value of suggestions.

11. The BEST general rule for a supervisor to follow in giving praise and criticism is to
    A. criticize and praise publicly
    B. criticize publicly and praise privately
    C. praise and criticize privately
    D. praise publicly and criticize privately

12. An important step in designing an error-control policy is to determine the maximum number of errors that can be considered acceptable for the entire organization.
    Of the following, the MOST important factor in making such a decision is the
    A. number of clerical staff available to check for errors
    B. frequency of errors by supervisors
    C. human and material costs of errors
    D. number of errors that will become known to the public

13. When a supervisor tries to correct a situation where errors have been widespread, he should concentrate his efforts, and those of the employees involved, on
    A. avoiding future mistakes   B. fixing appropriate blame
    C. preparing a written report   D. determining fair penalties

14. When delegating work to a subordinate, a supervisor should ALWAYS tell the subordinate
    A. each step in the procedure for doing the work
    B. how much time to expend
    C. what is to be accomplished
    D. whether reports are necessary

15. The responsibilities of all employees should be clearly defined and understood. In addition, in order for employees to successfully fulfill their responsibilities, they should also GENERALLY be given
    A. written directives   B. close supervision
    C. corresponding authority   D. daily instructions

16. The one of the following types of training in which positive transfer of training to the actual work situation is MOST likely to take place is _____ training.
    A. conference   B. demonstration
    C. classroom   D. on-the-job

17. The type of training or instruction in which the subject matter is presented in small units called frames is known as
    A. programmed instruction
    B. reinforcement
    C. remediation
    D. skills training

18. In order to bring about maximum learning in a training situation, a supervisor acting as a trainer should attempt to create a setting in which
    A. all trainees experience a large amount of failure as an incentive
    B. all trainees experience a small amount of failure as an incentive
    C. each trainee experiences approximately the same amounts of success and failure
    D. each trainee experiences as much success and as little failure as possible

19. Assume that, in a training course given by an agency, the instructor conducts a brief quiz, on paper, toward the close of each session.
    From the point of view of maximizing learning, it would be BEST for the instructor to
    A. wait until the last session to provide the correct answers
    B. give the correct answers aloud immediately after each quiz
    C. permit trainees to take the questions home with them so that they can look up the answers
    D. wait until the next session to provide the correct answers

20. A supervisor, in the course of evaluating employees, should ALWAYS determine whether
    A. employees realize that their work is under scrutiny
    B. the ratings will be included in permanent records
    C. employees meet standards of performance
    D. his statements on the rating form are similar to those made by the previous supervisor

21. All of the following are legitimate objectives of employee performance reporting systems EXCEPT
    A. serving as a check on personnel policies such as job qualification requirements and placement techniques
    B. determining who is the least efficient worker among a large number of employees
    C. improving employee performance by identifying strong and weak points in individual performance
    D. developing standards of satisfactory performance

22. Studies of existing employee performance evaluation schemes have revealed a common tendency to construct guides in order to measure <u>inferred</u> traits.
    Of the following, the BEST example of an inferred trait is
    A. appearance   B. loyalty   C. accuracy   D. promptness

23. Which of the following is MOST likely to be a positive influence in promoting common agreement at a staff conference?
    A. A mature, tolerant group of participants
    B. A strong chairman with firm opinions
    C. The normal differences of human personalities
    D. The urge to forcefully support one's views

24. Before holding a problem-solving conference, the conference leader sent to each invitee an announcement on which he listed the names of all invitees. His action in listing the names was
    A. *wise*, mainly because all invitees will know who has been invited, and can, if necessary, plan a proper approach
    B. *unwise*, mainly because certain invitees could form factions prior to the conference
    C. *unwise*, mainly because invitees might come to the conference in a belligerent mood if they had had interpersonal conflicts with other invitees
    D. *wise*, mainly because invitees who are antagonistic to each other could decide not to attend

25. Methods analysis is a detailed study of existing or proposed work methods for the purpose of improving agency operations.
    Of the following, it is MOST accurate to say that this type of study
    A. can sometimes be made informally by the experienced supervisor who can identify problems and suggest solutions
    B. is not suitable for studying the operations of a public agency
    C. will be successfully accomplished only if an outside organization reviews agency operations
    D. usually costs more to complete than is justified by the potential economies to be realized

KEY (CORRECT ANSWERS)

1.	D		11.	D
2.	C		12.	C
3.	B		13.	A
4.	A		14.	C
5.	B		15.	C
6.	C		16.	D
7.	B		17.	A
8.	C		18.	D
9.	B		19.	B
10.	D		20.	C
		21.		
		22.	B	
		23.	A	
		24.	A	
		25.	A	

TEST 2

DIRECTIONS: Each question or incomplete statement is followed by several suggested answers or completions. Select the one that BEST answers the question or completes the statement. *PRINT THE LETTER OF THE CORRECT ANSWER IN THE SPACE AT THE RIGHT.*

1. Present-day managerial practices advocate that adequate hierarchical levels of communication be maintained among all levels of management.
   Of the following, the BEST way to accomplish this is with
   A. intradepartmental memoranda only
   B. interdepartmental memoranda only
   C. periodic staff meetings, interdepartmental and intradepartmental memoranda
   D. interdepartmental and intradepartmental memoranda

   1.____

2. It is generally agreed upon that it is important to have effective communications in the unit so that everyone knows exactly what is expected of him.
   Of the following, the communications system which can assist in fulfilling this objective BEST is one which consists of
   A. written policies and procedures for administrative functions and verbal policies and procedures for professional functions
   B. written policies and procedures for professional and administrative functions
   C. verbal policies and procedures for professional and administrative functions
   D. verbal policies and procedures for professional functions

   2.____

3. If a department manager wishes to build an effective department, he MOST generally must
   A. be able to hire and fire as he feels necessary
   B. consider the total aspects of his job, his influence and the effects of his decisions
   C. have access to reasonable amounts of personnel and money with which to build his programs
   D. attend as many professional conferences as possible so that he can keep up-to-date with all the latest advances in the field

   3.____

4. Of the following, the factor which generally contributes MOST effectively to the performance of the unit is that the supervisor
   A. personally inspect the work of all employees
   B. fill orders at a faster rate than his subordinates
   C. have an exact knowledge of theory
   D. implement a program of professional development for his staff

   4.____

5. Administrative policies relate MOST closely to
   A. control of commodities and personnel
   B. general policies emanating from the central office
   C. fiscal management of the department only
   D. handling and dispensing of funds

   5.____

6. Part of being a good supervisor is to be able to develop an attitude towards employees which will motivate them to do their best on the job.
   The GOOD supervisor, therefore, should
   A. take an interest in subordinates, but not develop an all-consuming attitude in this area
   B. remain in an aloof position when dealing with employees
   C. be as close to subordinates as possible on the job
   D. take a complete interest in all the activities of subordinates, both on and off the job

7. The practice of a supervisor assigning an experienced employee to train new employees instead of training them himself is GENERALLY considered
   A. *undesirable*; the more experienced employee will resent being taken away from his regular job
   B. *desirable*; the supervisor can then devote more time to his regular duties
   C. *undesirable*; the more experienced employee is not working at the proper level to train new employees
   D. *desirable*; the more experienced employee is probably a better trainer than the supervisor

8. It is generally agreed that on-the-job training is MOST effective when new employees are
   A. provided with study manuals, standard operating procedures and other written materials to be studied for at least two weeks before the employees attempt to do the job
   B. shown how to do the job in detail, and then instructed to do the work under close supervision
   C. trained by an experienced worker for at least a week to make certain that the employees can do the job
   D. given work immediately which is checked at the end of each day

9. Employees sometimes form small informal groups, commonly called cliques. With regard to the effect of such groups on processing of the workload, the attitude a supervisor should take towards these cliques is that of
   A. *acceptance*, since they take the employees' minds off their work without wasting too much time
   B. *rejection*, since those workers inside the clique tend to do less work than the outsiders
   C. *acceptance*, since the supervisor is usually included in the clique
   D. *rejection*, since they are usually disliked by higher management

10. Of the following, the BEST statement regarding rules and regulations in a unit is that they
    A. are "necessary evils" to be tolerated by those at and above the first supervisory level only
    B. are stated in broad, indefinite terms so as to allow maximum amount of leeway in complying with them

C. must be understood by all employees in the unit
D. are primarily for management's needs since insurance regulations mandate them

11. It is sometimes considered desirable for a supervisor to survey the opinions of his employees before taking action on decisions affecting them.
    Of the following the greatest DISADVANTAGE of following this approach is that the employees might
    A. use this opportunity to complain rather than to make constructive suggestions
    B. lose respect for their supervisor whom they feel cannot make his own decisions
    C. regard this as an attempt by the supervisor to get ideas for which he can later claim credit
    D. be resentful if their suggestions are not adopted

12. Of the following, the MOST important reason for keeping statements of duties of employees up-to-date is to
    A. serve as a basis of information for other governmental jurisdictions
    B. enable the department of personnel to develop job-related examinations
    C. differentiate between levels within the occupational groups
    D. enable each employee to know what his duties are

13. Of the following, the BEST way to evaluate the progress of a new subordinate is to
    A. compare the output of the new employee from week to week as to quantity and quality
    B. obtain the opinions of the new employee's co-workers
    C. test the new employee periodically to see how much he has learned
    D. hold frequent discussions with the employee focusing on his work

14. Of the following, a supervisor is LEAST likely to contribute to good morale in the unit if he
    A. encourages employees to increase their knowledge and proficiency in their work on their own time
    B. reprimands subordinates uniformly when infractions are committed
    C. refuses to accept explanations for mistakes regardless of who has made them or how serious they are
    D. compliments subordinates for superior work performance in the presence of their peers

15. The practice of promoting supervisors from within a given unit only, rather than from within the entire agency, may BEST be described as
    A. *desirable*, because the type of work in each unit generally is substantially different from all other units
    B. *undesirable*, since it will severely reduce the number of eligible from which to select a supervisor

C. *desirable*, since it enables each employee to know in advance the precise extent of promotion opportunities in his unit
D. *undesirable*, because it creates numerous administrative and budgetary difficulties

16. Of the following, the BEST way for a supervisor to make assignments GENERALLY is to
    A. give the easier assignments to employees with greater seniority
    B. give the difficult assignments to the employees with greater seniority
    C. make assignments according to the ability of each employee
    D. rotate the assignments among the employees

17. Assume that a supervisor makes a proposal through appropriate channels which would delegate final authority and responsibility to a subordinate employee for a major control function within the agency.
    According to current management theory, this proposal should be
    A. *adopted*, since this would enable the supervisor to devote more time to non-routine tasks
    B. *rejected*, since final responsibility for this high-level assignment may not properly be delegated to a subordinate employee
    C. *adopted*, since the assignment of increased responsibility to subordinate employees is a vital part of their development and training
    D. *rejected*, since the morale of the subordinate employees not selected for this assignment would be adversely affected

18. If it becomes necessary for a supervisor to improve the performance of a subordinate to assure the achievement of results according to plans, the BEST course of action, of the following, generally would be to
    A. emphasize the subordinate's strengths and try to motivate the employee to improve on those factors
    B. emphasize the subordinate's weak areas of performance and try to bring them up to an acceptable standard
    C. issue a memorandum to all employees warning that if performance does not improve, disciplinary measures will be taken
    D. transfer the subordinate to another section engaged in different work

19. A supervisor who specifies each phase of a job in detail supervises closely and permits very little discretion in performance of tasks GENERALLY
    A. provides motivation for his staff to produce more work
    B. finds that his subordinate make fewer mistakes than those with minimal supervision
    C. finds that his subordinates have little or no incentive to work any harder than necessary
    D. provides superior training opportunities for his employees

20. Assume that you supervise two employees who do not get along well with each other. Their relationship has been continuously deteriorating. You decide to take steps to solve this problem by first determining the reason for their inability to get along with each other.
    This course of action is
    A. *desirable*, because their work is probably adversely affected by their differences
    B. *undesirable*, because your inquiries might be misinterpreted by the employees and cause resentment
    C. *desirable*, because you could then learn who is at fault for causing the deteriorating relationship and take appropriate disciplinary measures
    D. *undesirable*, because it is best to let them work their differences out between themselves

21. Routine procedures that have worked well in the past should be reviewed periodically by a supervisor MAINLY because
    A. they may have become outdated or in need of revision
    B. employees may dislike the procedures even though they have proven successful in the past
    C. these reviews are the main part of a supervisor's job
    D. this practice serves to give the supervisor an idea of how productive his subordinates are

22. Assume that an employee tells his supervisor about a grievance he has against a co-worker. The supervisor assures the employee that he will immediately take action to eliminate the grievance.
    The supervisor's attitude should be considered
    A. *correct*, because a good supervisor is one who can come to a quick decision
    B. *incorrect*, because the supervisor should have told the employee that he will investigate the grievance and then determine a future course of action
    C. *correct*, because the employee's morale will be higher, resulting in greater productivity
    D. *incorrect*, because the supervisor should remain uninvolved and let the employees settle grievances between themselves

23. If an employee's work output is low and of poor quality due to faulty work habits, the MOST constructive of the following ways for a supervisor to correct this situation *generally* is to
    A. discipline the employee
    B. transfer the employee to another unit
    C. provide additional training
    D. check the employee's work continuously

24. Assume that it becomes necessary for a supervisor to ask his staff to work overtime.
    Which one of the following techniques is MOST likely to win their willing cooperation to do this?

A. Point out that this is part of their job specification entitled "performs related work"
B. Explain the reason it is necessary for the employees to work overtime
C. Promise the employees special consideration regarding future leave matters
D. Warn that if the employees do not work overtime, they will face possible disciplinary action

25. If an employee's work performance has recently fallen below established minimum standards for quality and quantity, the threat of demotion or other disciplinary measures as an attempt to improve this employee's performance would probably be the MOST acceptable and effective course of action
   A. *only* after other more constructive measures have failed
   B. *if* applied uniformly to all employees as soon as performance falls below standard
   C. *only* if the employee understands that the threat will not actually be carried out
   D. *if* the employee is promised that, as soon as his work performance improves, he will be reinstated to his previous status

KEY (CORRECT ANSWERS)

1.	C		11.	D
2.	B		12.	D
3.	B		13.	A
4.	D		14.	C
5.	A		15.	B
6.	A		16.	C
7.	B		17.	B
8.	B		18.	B
9.	A		19.	C
10.	C		20.	A

21.	A
22.	B
23.	C
24.	B
25.	A

TEST 3

DIRECTIONS: Each question or incomplete statement is followed by several suggested answers or completions. Select the one that BEST answers the question or completes the statement. *PRINT THE LETTER OF THE CORRECT ANSWER IN THE SPACE AT THE RIGHT.*

1. If, as a supervisor, it becomes necessary for you to assign an employee to supervise your unit during your vacation, it would generally be BEST to select the employee who
    A. is the best technician on the staff
    B. can get the work out smoothly, without friction
    C. has the most seniority
    D. is the most popular with the group

    1._____

2. Assume that, as a supervisor, your own work has accumulated to the point where you decide that it is desirable for you to delegate in order to meet your deadlines.
    The one of the following tasks which would be MOST appropriate to delegate to a subordinate is
    A. checking the work of the employees for accuracy
    B. attending a staff conference at which implementation of a new departmental policy will be discussed
    C. preparing a final report including a recommendation on purchase of expensive new laboratory equipment
    D. preparing final budget estimates for next year's budget

    2._____

3. Of the following actions, the one LEAST appropriate for you to take during an initial interview with a new employee is to
    A. find out about the experience and education of the new employee
    B. attempt to determine for what job in your unit the employee would best be suited
    C. tell the employee about his duties and responsibilities
    D. ascertain whether the employee will make good promotion material

    3._____

4. If it becomes necessary to reprimand a subordinate employee, the BEST of the following ways to do this is to
    A. ask the employee to stay after working hours and then reprimand him
    B. reprimand the employee immediately after the infraction has been committed
    C. take the employee aside and speak to him privately during regular working hours
    D. write a short memo to the employee warning that strict adherence to departmental policy and procedures is required of all employees

    4._____

5. If you, as a supervisor, believe that one of your subordinate employees has a serious problem, such as alcoholism or an emotional disturbance, which is adversely affecting his work, the BEST way to handle this situation *initially* would be to

    5._____

A. urge him to seek proper professional help before he is dismissed from his job
B. ignore it and let the employee work out the problem himself
C. suggest that the employee take an extended leave of absence until he can again function effectively
D. frankly tell the employee that unless his work improves, you will take disciplinary measures against him

6. Of the following, the BEST way to develop a subordinate's potential is to
   A. give him a fair chance to learn by doing
   B. assign him more than his share of work
   C. criticize only his work
   D. urge him to do his work rapidly

7. During a survey, an employee from another agency asks you to assist him on a job which would require a full day of your time.
   Of the following, the BEST immediate action for you to take is to
   A. refuse to assist him
   B. ask for compensation before doing it
   C. assist him promptly
   D. notify his department head

8. Of the following, the BEST way to handle an overly talkative subordinate is to
   A. have your superior talk to him about it
   B. have a subordinate talk to him about it
   C. talk to him about it in a group conference
   D. talk to him about it in private

9. While you are making a survey, a citizen questions you about the work you are doing.
   Of the following, the BEST thing to do is to
   A. answer the questions tactfully
   B. refuse to answer any questions
   C. advise him to write a letter to the main office
   D. answer the questions in double-talk

10. Respect for a supervisor is MOST likely to increase if he is
    A. morose   B. sporadic   C. vindictive   D. zealous

11. A subordinate who continuously bypasses his immediate supervisor for technical information should be
    A. reprimanded by his immediate supervisor
    B. ignored by his immediate supervisor
    C. given more difficult work to do
    D. given less difficult work to do

12. Complicated instructions should NOT be written
    A. accurately   B. lucidly   C. factually   D. verbosely

13. Of the following, the MOST important reason for checking a report is to
    A. check accuracy
    B. eliminate unnecessary sections
    C. catch mistakes
    D. check for delineation

13.____

14. Two subordinates under your supervision dislike each other to the extent that production is cut down.
    Your BEST action as a supervisor is to
    A. ignore the matter and hope for the best
    B. transfer the more aggressive man
    C. cut down on the workload
    D. talk to them together about the matter

14.____

15. One of the following characteristics which a supervisor should NOT display while explaining a job to a subordinate is
    A. enthusiasm   B. confidence   C. apathy   D. determination

15.____

16. Of the following, for BEST production of work, it should be assigned according to a person's
    A. attitude toward the work
    B. ability to do the work
    C. salary
    D. seniority

16.____

17. You receive an anonymous written complaint from a citizen about a subordinate who used abusive language.
    Of the following, your BEST course of action is to
    A. ignore the letter
    B. report it to your supervisor
    C. discuss the complaint with the subordinate privately
    D. keep the subordinate in the office

17.____

18. A supervisor should recognize that the way to get the BEST results from his instructions and assignments to the staff is to use
    A. a suggestive approach after he has decided exactly what is to be done and how
    B. the willing and cooperative staff members and avoid the hard-to-handle people
    C. care to select the persons most capable of carrying out the assignments
    D. an authoritative, non-nonsense tone when issuing instructions or giving assignments

18.____

19. As the supervisor of a unit, you find that you are spending too much of your time on routine tasks and not enough on coordinating the work of the staff or preparing necessary reports.
    Of the following, it would be MOST advisable for you to
    A. discard a great portion of the routine jobs done in the unit
    B. give some of the routine jobs to other members of the staff
    C. postpone the routine jobs and concentrate on coordinating the work of the staff
    D. delegate the job of coordinating the work to the most capable member of the staff

19.____

20. At times a supervisor may be called upon to train new employees. Suppose that you are giving such training in several sessions to be held on different days. During the first session, a trainee interrupts several times to ask questions at key points in your discussion.
Of the following, the BEST way to handle this trainee is to
    A. advise him to pay closer attention so he can avoid asking too many questions
    B. tell him to listen without interrupting and he'll hear his questions answered
    C. answer his questions to show him that you know your field, but make a mental note that this trainee is a troublemaker
    D. answer each question fully and make certain he understands the answers

21. Employee errors can be reduced to a minimum by effective supervision and by training.
Which of the following approaches used by a supervisor would usually be MOST effective in handling an employee who has made an avoidable and serious error for the first time?
    A. Tell the worker how other employees avoid making errors
    B. Analyze with the employee the situation leading to the error and then take whatever administrative or training steps are needed to avoid such errors
    C. Use this error as the basis for a staff meeting at which the employee's error is disclosed and discussed in an effort to improve the performance
    D. Urge the employee to modify his behavior in light of his mistake

22. Suppose that a particular staff member, formerly one of your most regular workers, has recently fallen into the habit of arriving a bit late to work several times a week. You feel that such a habit can grow consistently worse and spread to other staff members unless it is checked.
Of the following, the BEST action for you to take, as the supervisor in charge of the unit, is to
    A. go immediately to your own supervisor, present the facts, and have this employee disciplined
    B. speak privately to this tardy employee, advise him of the need to improve his punctuality, and inform him that he'll be disciplined if late again
    C. talk to the co-worker with whom this late employee is most friendly, and ask the friend to help him solve his tardiness problem
    D. speak privately with this employee, and try to discover and deal with the reasons for the latenesses

23. A supervisor may make an assignment in the form of a request, a command, or a call for volunteers.
It is LEAST desirable to make an assignment in the form of a request when
    A. an employee does not like the particular kind of assignment to be given
    B. the assignment requires working past the regular closing day
    C. an emergency has come up
    D. the assignment is not particularly pleasant for anybody

24. When you give a certain task that you normally perform yourself to one of your employees, it is MOST important that you
    A. lead the employee to believe that he has been chosen above others to perform this job
    B. describe the job as important even though it is merely a routine task
    C. explain the job that needs to be accomplished, but always let the employee decide how to do it
    D. tell the employee why you are delegating the job to him and explain exactly what he is to do

25. A supervisor when instructing new trainees in the routine of his unit should include a description of the department's overall objectives and programs in order to
    A. insure that individual work assignments will be completed satisfactorily
    B. create a favorable impression of his supervisory capabilities
    C. develop a better understanding of the purposes behind work assignments
    D. produce an immediate feeling of group cooperation

KEY (CORRECT ANSWERS)

1.	B		11.	A
2.	A		12.	D
3.	D		13.	C
4.	C		14.	D
5.	A		15.	C
6.	A		16.	B
7.	A		17.	C
8.	D		18.	C
9.	A		19.	B
10.	D		20.	D

21.	B
22.	D
23.	A
24.	D
25.	C

TEST 4

DIRECTIONS: Each question or incomplete statement is followed by several suggested answers or completions. Select the one that BEST answers the question or completes the statement. *PRINT THE LETTER OF THE CORRECT ANSWER IN THE SPACE AT THE RIGHT.*

1. An integral part of every supervisor's job is getting his ideas or instructions across to his staff.
   The extent of his success, if he has a reasonably competent staff, is PRIMARILY dependent on the
   A. interest of the employee
   B. intelligence of the employee
   C. reasoning behind the ideas or instructions
   D. presentation of the ideas or instructions

   1.____

2. Generally, what is the FIRST action the supervisor should take when an employee approaches him with a complaint?
   A. Review the employee's recent performance with him
   B. Use the complaint as a basis to discuss improvement of procedures
   C. Find out from the employee the details of the complaint
   D. Advise the employee to take his complaint to the head of the department

   2.____

3. Of the following, which is NOT usually considered one of the purposes of counseling an employee after an evaluation of his performance?
   A. Explaining the performance standards used by the supervisor
   B. Discussing necessary discipline action to be taken
   C. Emphasizing the employee's strengths and weaknesses
   D. Planning better utilization of the employee's strengths

   3.____

4. Assume that a supervisor, when reviewing a decision reached by one of his subordinates, finds the decision incorrect.
   Under these circumstances, it would be MOST desirable for the supervisor to
   A. correct the decision and inform the subordinate of this at a staff meeting
   B. correct the decision and suggest a more detailed analysis in the future
   C. help the employee find the reason for the correct decision
   D. refrain from assigning this type of a problem to the employee

   4.____

5. An IMPORTANT characteristic of a good supervisor is his ability to
   A. be a stern disciplinarian   B. put off the settling of grievances
   C. solve problems   D. find fault in individuals

   5.____

6. A new supervisor will BEST obtain the respect of the men assigned to him if he
   A. makes decisions rapidly and sticks to the, regardless of whether they are right or wrong
   B. makes decisions rapidly and then changes them just as rapidly if the decisions are wrong
   C. does not make any decisions unless he is absolutely sure that they are right
   D. makes his decisions after considering carefully all available information

   6.____

7. A newly appointed worker is operating at a level of performance below that of the other employees.
In this situation, a supervisor should FIRST
    A. lower the acceptable standard for the new man
    B. find out why the new man cannot do as well as the others
    C. advise the new worker he will be dropped from the payroll at the end of the probationary period
    D. assign another new worker to assist the first man

8. Assume that you have to instruct a new man on a specific departmental operation. The new man seems unsure of what you have said.
Of the following, the BEST way for you to determine whether the man has understood you is to
    A. have the man explain the operation to you in his own words
    B. repeat your explanation to him slowly
    C. repeat your explanation to him, using simpler wording
    D. emphasize the important parts of the operation to him

9. A supervisor realizes that he has taken an instantaneous dislike to a new worker assigned to him.
The BEST course of action for the supervisor to take in this case is to
    A. be especially observant of the new worker's actions
    B. request that the new worker be reassigned
    C. make a special effort to be fair to the new worker
    D. ask to be transferred himself

10. A supervisor gives detailed instructions to his men as to how a certain type of job is to be done.
One ADVANTAGE of this practice is that this will
    A. result in a more flexible operation
    B. standardize operations
    C. encourage new men to learn
    D. encourage initiative to learn

11. Of the following the one that would MOST likely be the result of poor planning is:
    A. Omissions are discovered after the work is completed
    B. During the course of normal inspection, a meter is found to be inaccessible
    C. An inspector completes his assignments for that day ahead of schedule
    D. A problem arises during an inspection and prevents an inspector from completing his day's assignments

12. Of the following, the BEST way for a supervisor to maintain good employee morale is for the supervisor to
    A. avoid correcting the employee when he makes mistakes
    B. continually praise the employee's work even when it is of average quality
    C. show that he is willing to assist in solving the employee's problems
    D. accept the employee's excuses for failure even though the excuses are not valid

13. A supervisor takes time to explain to his men why a departmental order has been issued.
    This practice is
    A. *good*, mainly because without this explanation the men will not be able to carry out the order
    B. *bad*, mainly because time will be wasted for no useful purpose
    C. *good*, because understanding the reasons behind an order will lead to more effective carrying out of the order
    D. *bad*, because men will then question every order that they receive

14. Of the following, the MOST important responsibility of a supervisor in charge of a section is to
    A. establish close personal relationships with each of his subordinates in the section
    B. insure that each subordinate in the section knows the full range of his duties and responsibilities
    C. maintain friendly relations with his immediate supervisor
    D. protect his subordinate from criticism from any source

15. The BEST way to get a good work output from employees is to
    A. hold over them the threat of disciplinary action or removal
    B. maintain a steady, unrelenting pressure on them
    C. show them that you can do anything they can do faster and better
    D. win their respect and liking, so they want to work for you

KEY (CORRECT ANSWERS)

1.	A	6.	D	11.	A
2.	C	7.	B	12.	C
3.	A	8.	A	13.	C
4.	C	9.	C	14.	B
5.	C	10.	B	15.	D

PREPARING WRITTEN MATERIAL
EXAMINATION SECTION
TEST 1

DIRECTIONS: Each of Questions 1 through 5 consists of a sentence which may or may not be an example of good formal English usage. Examine each sentence, considering grammar, punctuation, spelling, capitalization, and awkwardness. Then choose the correct statement about it from the four options below it. If the English usage in the sentence given is better than any of the changes suggested in options B, C, or D, pick option A. (Do not pick an option that will change the meaning of the sentence.) *PRINT THE LETTER OF THE CORRECT ANSWER IN THE SPACE AT THE RIGHT.*

1. I don't know who could possibly of broken it.
   A. This is an example of good formal English usage.
   B. The word "who" should be replaced by the word "whom."
   C. The word "of" should be replaced by the word "have."
   D. The word "broken" should be replaced by the word "broke."

2. Telephoning is easier than to write.
   A. This is an example of good formal English usage.
   B. The word "telephoning" should be spelled "telephoneing."
   C. The word "than" should be replaced by the word "then."
   D. The words "to write" should be replaced by the word "writing."

3. The two operators who have been assigned to these consoles are on vacation.
   A. This is an example of good formal English usage.
   B. A comma should be placed after the word "operators."
   C. The word "who" should be replaced by the word "whom."
   D. The word "are" should be replaced by the word "is."

4. You were suppose to teach me how to operate a plugboard.
   A. This is an example of good formal English usage.
   B. The word "were" should be replaced by the word "was."
   C. The word "suppose" should be replaced by the word "supposed."
   D. The word "teach" should be replaced by the word "learn."

5. If you had taken my advice; you would have spoken with him.
   A. This is an example of good formal English usage.
   B. The word "advice" should be spelled "advise."
   C. The words "had taken" should be replaced by the word "take."
   D. The semicolon should be changed to a comma.

KEY (CORRECT ANSWERS)

1. C
2. D
3. A
4. C
5. D

TEST 2

DIRECTIONS: Select the correct answer. *PRINT THE LETTER OF THE CORRECT ANSWER IN THE SPACE AT THE RIGHT.*

1. The one of the following sentences which is MOST acceptable from the viewpoint of correct grammatical usage is:
    A. I do not know which action will have worser results.
    B. He should of known better.
    C. Both the officer on the scene, and his immediate supervisor, is charged with the responsibility.
    D. An officer must have initiative because his supervisor will not always be available to answer questions.

    1._____

2. The one of the following sentences which is MOST acceptable from the viewpoint of correct grammatical usage is:
    A. Of all the officers available, the better one for the job will be picked.
    B. Strict orders were given to all the officers, except he.
    C. Study of the law will enable you to perform your duties more efficiently.
    D. It seems to me that you was wrong in failing to search the two men.

    2._____

3. The one of the following sentences which does NOT contain a misspelled word is:
    A. The duties you will perform are similar to the duties of a patrolman.
    B. Officers must be constantly alert to sieze the initiative.
    C. Officers in this organization are not entitled to special privileges.
    D. Any changes in procedure will be announced publically.

    3._____

4. The one of the following sentences which does NOT contain a misspelled word is:
    A. It will be to your advantage to keep your firearm in good working condition.
    B. There are approximately fourty men on sick leave.
    C. Your first duty will be to pursuade the person to obey the law.
    D. Fires often begin in flameable material kept in lockers.

    4._____

5. The one of the following sentences which does NOT contain a misspelled word is:
    A. Offices are not required to perform technical maintainance.
    B. He violated the regulations on two occasions.
    C. Every employee will be held responable for errors.
    D. This was his nineth absence in a year.

    5._____

KEY (CORRECT ANSWERS)

1. D
2. C
3. C
4. A
5. B

TEST 3

DIRECTIONS: Select the correct answer. *PRINT THE LETTER OF THE CORRECT ANSWER IN THE SPACE AT THE RIGHT.*

1. You are answering a letter that was written on the letterhead of the ABC Company and signed by James H. Wood, Treasurer.
   What is usually considered to be the correct salutation to use in your reply?
   A. Dear ABC Company:
   B. Dear Sirs:
   C. Dear Mr. Wood:
   D. Dear Mr. Treasurer:

   1.____

2. Assume that one of your duties is to handle routine letters of inquiry from the public.
   The one of the following which is usually considered to be MOST desirable in replying to such a letter is a
   A. detailed answer handwritten on the original letter of inquiry
   B. phone call, since you can cover details more easily over the phone than in a letter
   C. short letter giving the specific information requested
   D. long letter discussing all possible aspects of the question raised

   2.____

3. The CHIEF reason for dividing a letter into paragraphs is to
   A. make the message clear to the reader by starting a new paragraph for each new topic
   B. make a short letter occupy as much of the page as possible
   C. keep the reader's attention by providing a pause from time to time
   D. make the letter look neat and businesslike

   3.____

4. Your superior has asked you to send an e-mail from your agency to a government agency in another city. He has written out the message and has indicated the name of the government agency.
   When you dictate the message to your secretary, which of the following items that your superior has NOT mentioned must you be sure to include?
   A. Today's date
   B. The full address of the government agency
   C. A polite opening such as "Dear Sirs"
   D. A final sentence such as "We would appreciate hearing from your agency in reply as soon as is convenient for you"

   4.____

5. The one of the following sentences which is grammatically preferable to the others is:
   A. Our engineers will go over your blueprints so that you may have no problems in construction.
   B. For a long time he had been arguing that we, not he, are to blame for the confusion.
   C. I worked on this automobile for two hours and still cannot find out what is wrong with it.
   D. Accustomed to all kinds of hardships, fatigue seldom bothers veteran policemen.

   5.____

KEY (CORRECT ANSWERS)

1. C
2. C
3. A
4. B
5. A

TEST 4

DIRECTIONS: Select the correct answer. *PRINT THE LETTER OF THE CORRECT ANSWER IN THE SPACE AT THE RIGHT.*

1. Suppose that an applicant for a job as snow laborer presents a letter from a former employer stating: "John Smith has a pleasing manner and never got into an argument with his fellow employees. He was never late or absent." This letter
   A. indicates that with some training Smith will make a good snow gang boss
   B. presents no definite evidence of Smith's ability to do snow work
   C. proves definitely that Smith has never done any snow work before
   D. proves definitely that Smith will do better than average work as a snow laborer

   1.____

2. Suppose you must write a letter to a local organization in your section refusing a request in connection with collection of their refuse.
   You should start the letter by
   A. explaining in detail the consideration you gave the request
   B. praising the organization for its service to the community
   C. quoting the regulation which forbids granting the request
   D. stating your regret that the request cannot be granted

   2.____

3. Suppose a citizen writes in for information as to whether or not he may sweep refuse into the gutter. A Sanitation officer answers as follows:
   Dear Sir:
   No person is permitted to litter, sweep, throw or cast, or direct, suffer or permit any person under his control to litter, sweep, throw or cast any ashes, garbage, paper, dust, or other rubbish or refuse into any public street or place, vacant lot, air shaft, areaway, backyard or court.
                                 Very truly yours,
                                 John Doe
   This letter is *poorly* written CHIEFLY because
   A. the opening is not indented   B. the thought is not clear
   C. the tone is too formal and cold   D. there are too many commas used

   3.____

4. A section of a disciplinary report written by a Sanitation officer states: "It is requested that subject Sanitation man be advised that his future activities be directed towards reducing his recurrent tardiness else disciplinary action will be initiated which may result in summary discharge."
   This section of the report is *poorly* written MAINLY because
   A. at least one word is misspelled   B. it is not simply expressed
   C. more than one idea is expressed   D. the purpose is not stated

   4.____

5. A section of a disciplinary report written by an officer states: "He comes in late. He takes too much time for lunch. He is lazy. I recommend his services be dispensed with."
   This section of the report is *poorly* written MAINLY because
   A. it ends with a preposition   B. it is not well organized
   C. no supporting facts are stated   D. the sentences are too simple

   5.____

KEY (CORRECT ANSWERS)

1. B
2. D
3. C
4. B
5. C

PREPARING WRITTEN MATERIAL

PARAGRAPH REARRANGEMENT
COMMENTARY

The sentences that follow are in scrambled order. You are to rearrange them in proper order and indicate the letter choice containing the correct answer at the space at the right.

Each group of sentences in this section is actually a paragraph presented in scrambled order. Each sentence in the group has a place in that paragraph; no sentence is to be left out. You are to read each group of sentences and decide upon the best order in which to put the sentences so as to form a well-organized paragraph.

The questions in this section measure the ability to solve a problem when all the facts relevant to its solution are not given.

More specifically, certain positions of responsibility and authority require the employee to discover connection between events sometimes, apparently, unrelated. In order to do this, the employee will find it necessary to correctly infer that unspecified events have probably occurred or are likely to occur. This ability becomes especially important when action must be taken on incomplete information.

Accordingly, these questions require competitors to choose among several suggested alternatives, each of which presents a different sequential arrangement of the events. Competitors must choose the MOST logical of the suggested sequences.

In order to do so, they may be required to draw on general knowledge to infer missing concepts or events that are essential to sequencing the given events. Competitors should be careful to infer only what is essential to the sequence. The plausibility of the wrong alternatives will always require the inclusion of unlikely events or of additional chains of events which are NOT essential to sequencing the given events.

It's very important to remember that you are looking for the best of the four possible choices, and that the best choice of all may not even be one of the answers you're given to choose from.

There is no one right way to solve these problems. Many people have found it helpful to first write out the order of the sentences, as they would have arranged them, on their scrap paper before looking at the possible answers. If their optimum answer is there, this can save them some time. If it isn't, this method can still give insight into solving the problem. Others find it most helpful to just go through each of the possible choices, contrasting each as they go along. You should use whatever method feels comfortable and works for you.

While most of these types of questions are not that difficult, we've added a higher percentage of the difficult type, just to give you more practice. Usually there are only one or two questions on this section that contain such subtle distinctions that you're unable to answer confidently. And you then may find yourself stuck deciding between two possible choices, neither of which you're sure about.

PREPARING WRITTEN MATERIAL
PARAGRAPH REARRANGEMENT
EXAMINATION SECTION
TEST 1

DIRECTIONS: The following groups of sentences need to be arranged in an order that makes sense. Select the letter preceding the sequence that represents the best sentence order. *PRINT THE LETTER OF THE CORRECT ANSWER IN THE SPACE AT THE RIGHT.*

1.
   I. The ostrich egg shell's legendary toughness makes it an excellent substitute for certain types of dishes or dinnerware, and in parts of Africa ostrich shells are cut and decorated for use as containers for water.
   II. Since prehistoric times, people have used the enormous egg of the ostrich as a part of their diet, a practice which has required much patience and hard work—to hard boil an ostrich egg takes about four hours.
   III. Opening the egg's shell, which is rock hard and nearly an inch thick, requires heavy tools, such as a saw or chisel; from inside, a baby ostrich must use a hornlike projection on its beak as a miniature pick-axe to escape from the egg.
   IV. The offspring of all higher-order animals originate from single egg cells that are carried by mothers, and most of these eggs are relatively small, often microscopic.
   V. The egg of the African ostrich, however, weighs a massive thirty pounds, making it the largest single cell on earth, and a common object of human curiosity and wonder.
   The BEST order is:
   A. V, IV, I, II, III   B. I, IV, V, III, II   C. IV, II, III, V, I   D. IV, V, II, III, I

   1.____

2.
   I. Typically only a few feet high on the open sea, individual tsunami have been known to circle the entire globe two or three times if their progress is not interrupted, but are not usually dangerous until they approach the shallow water that surrounds land masses.
   II. Some of the most terrifying and damaging hazards caused by earthquakes are tsunami, which were once called "tidal waves"—a poorly chosen name, since these waves have nothing to do with tides.
   III. Then a wave, slowed by the sudden drag on the lower part of its moving water column, will pile upon itself, sometimes reaching a height of over 100 feet.
   IV. Tsunami (Japanese for "great harbor wave") are seismic waves that are caused by earthquakes near oceanic trenches, and once triggered, can travel up to 600 miles an hour on the open ocean.
   V. A land-shoaling tsunami is capable of extraordinary destruction; some tsunami have deposited large boats miles inland, washed out two-foot-thick seawalls, and scattered locomotive trains over long distances.
   The BEST order is:
   A. IV, I, III, II, V   B. I, III, IV, II, V   C. V, I, III, II, IV   D. II, IV, I, III, V

   2.____

3.
I. Soon, by the 1940s, jazz was the most popular type of music among American intellectuals and college students.
II. In the early days of jazz, it was considered "lowdown" music, or music that was played only in rough, disreputable bars and taverns.
III. However, jazz didn't take too long to develop from early ragtime melodies into more complex, sophisticated forms, such as Charlie Parker's "bebop" style of jazz.
IV. After charismatic band leaders such as Duke Ellington and Count Basie brought jazz to a larger audience, and jazz continued to evolve into more complicated forms, white audiences began to accept and even to enjoy the new American art form.
V. Many white Americans, who then dictated the tastes of society, were wary of music that was played almost exclusively in black clubs in the poorer sections of cities and towns.

The BEST order is:
A. V, IV, III, II, I   B. II, V, III, IV, I   C. IV, V, III, I, II   D. I, II, IV, III, V

4.
I. Then, hanging in a windless place, the magnetized end of the needle would always point to the south.
II. The needle could then be balanced on the rim of a cup, or the edge of a fingernail, but this balancing act was hard to maintain, and the needle often fell off.
III. Other needles would point to the north, and it was important for any traveler finding his way with a compass to remember which kind of magnetized needle he was carrying.
IV. To make some of the earliest compasses in recorded history, ancient Chinese "magicians" would rub a needle with a piece of magnetized iron called a lodestone.
V. A more effective method of keeping the needle free to swing with its magnetic pull was to attach a strand of silk to the center of the needle with a tiny piece of wax.

The BEST order is:
A. IV, II, V, I, III   B. IV, III, V, II, I   C. IV, V, II, I, III   D. IV, I, III, V, II

5.
I. The now-famous first mate of the *H.M.S. Bounty*, Fletcher Christian, founded one of the world's most peculiar civilizations in 1790.
II. The men knew they had just committed a crime for which they could be hanged, so they set sail for Pitcairn, a remote, abandoned island in the far eastern region of the Polynesian archipelago, accompanied by twelve Polynesian women and six men.
III. In a mutiny that has become legendary, Christian and the others forced Captain Bligh into a lifeboat and set him adrift off the coast of Tonga in April of 1789.
IV. In early 1790, the *Bounty* landed at Pitcairn Island, where the men lived out the rest of their lives and founded an isolated community which to this day includes direct descendants of Christian and the other Crewmen.

V. The *Bounty*, commanded by Captain William Bligh, was in the middle of a global voyage, and Christian and his shipmates had come to the conclusion that Bligh was a reckless madman who would lead them to their deaths unless they took the ship from him.
The BEST order is:
   A. IV, V, III, II, I   B. I, III, V, II, IV   C. I, V, III, II, IV   D. III, I, V, IV, II

6.
  I. But once the vines had been led to make orchids, the flowers had to be carefully hand-pollinated, because unpollinated orchids usually lasted less than a day, wilting and dropping off the vine before it had even become dark.
  II. The Totonac farmers discovered that looping a vine back around once it reached a five-foot height on its host tree would cause the vine to flower.
  III. Though they knew how to process the fruit pods and extract vanilla's flavoring agent, the Totonacs also knew that a wild vanilla vine did not produce abundant flowers or fruit.
  IV. Wild vines climbed along the trunks and canopies of trees, and this constant upward growth diverted most of the vine's energy to making leaves instead of the orchid flowers that once pollinated, would produce the flavorful pods.
  V. Hundreds of years before vanilla became a prized food flavoring in Europe and the Western World, the Totonac Indians of the Mexican Gulf Coast were skilled cultivators of the vanilla vine, whose fruit they literally worshipped as a goddess.
The BEST order is:
   A. II, III, IV, I, V   B. II, IV, III, I, V   C. V, III, IV, II, I   D. III, IV, I, II, V

7.
  I. Once airborne, the spider is at the mercy of the air currents—usually the spider takes a brief journey, traveling close to the ground, but some have been found in air samples collected as high as 10,000 feet, or been reported landing on ships far out at sea.
  II. Once a young spider has hatched, it must leave the environment into which it was born as quickly as possible, in order to avoid competing with its hundreds of brothers and sisters for food.
  III. The silk rises into warm air currents, and as soon as the pull feels adequate the spider lets go and drifts up into the air, suspended from the silk strand in the same way that a person might parasail.
  IV. To help young spiders do this, many species have adapted a practice known as "aerial dispersal," or, in common speech, "ballooning."
  V. A spider that wants to leave its surroundings quickly will climb to the top of a grass system or twig, face into the wind, and aim its back end into the air, releasing a long stream of silk from the glands near the tip of its abdomen.
The BEST order is:
   A. V, IV, II, III, I   B. V, II, IV, I, III   C. II, V, IV, III, I   D. II, IV, V, III, I

8. I. For about a year, Tycho worked at a castle in Prague with a scientist named Johannes Kepler, but their association was cut short by another argument that drove Kepler out of the castle, to later develop, on his own, the theory of planetary orbits.
    II. Tycho found life without a nose embarrassing, so he made a new nose for himself out of silver, which reportedly remained glued to his face for the rest of his life.
    III. Tycho Brahe, the 17th-century Danish astronomer, is today more famous for his odd and arrogant personality than for any contribution he has made to our knowledge of the stars and planets.
    IV. Early in his career, as a student at Rostock University, Tycho got into an argument with another student about who was the better mathematician, and the two became so angry that the argument turned into a sword fight, during which Tycho's nose was sliced off.
    V. Later in his life, Tycho's arrogance may have kept him from playing a part in one of the greatest astronomical discoveries in history: the elliptical orbits of the solar system's planets.
    The BEST order is:
    A. I, IV, II, III, V   B. IV, II, III, V, I   C. IV, II, I, III, V   D. III, IV, II, V, I

9. I. The processionaries are so used to this routine that if a person picks up the end of a silk line and brings it back to the origin—creating a closed circle—the caterpillars may travel around and around for days, sometimes starving or freezing, without changing course.
    II. Rather than relying on sight or sound, the other caterpillars, who are lined up end-to-end behind the leader, travel to and from their nests by walking on this silk line, and each will reinforce it by laying down its own marking line as it passes over.
    III. In order to insure the safety of individuals, the processionary caterpillar nests in a tree with dozens of other caterpillars, and at night, when it is safest, they all leave together in search of food.
    IV. The processionary caterpillar of the European continent is a perfect illustration of how much some inspect species rely on instinct in their daily routines.
    V. As they leave their nests, the processionaries form a single-file line behind a leader who spins and lays out a silk line to mark the chosen path.
    The BEST order is:
    A. IV, III, V, II, I   B. III, V, IV, II, I   C. III, V, II, I, IV   D. IV, V, III, I, II

10. I. Often, the child is also given a handcrafted walker or push cart, to provide support for its first upright explorations.
    II. In traditional Indian families, a child's first steps are celebrated as a ceremonial event, rooted in ancient myth.
    III. These carts are often intricately designed to resemble the chariot of Krishna, an important figure in Indian mythology.
    IV. The sound of these anklet bells is intended to mimic the footsteps of the legendary child Rama, who is celebrated in devotional songs throughout India.

V. When the child's parents see that the child is ready to begin walking, they will fit it with specially designed ankle bracelets, adorned with gently ringing bells.

The BEST order is:
A. II, III, IV, I, V   B. II, V, III, I, IV   C. V, IV, I, III, II   D. V, III, II, I, IV

11. I. The settlers planted Osage oranges all across Middle America, and today long lines and rectangles of Osage orange trees can still be seen on the prairies, running along the former boundaries of farms that no longer exist.
    II. After trying sod walls and water-filled ditches with no success, American farmers began to look for a plant that was adaptable to prairie weather, and that could be trimmed into a hedge that was "pig-tight, horse-high, and bull-strong."
    III. The tree, so named because it bore a large (but inedible) fruit the size of an orange, was among the sturdiest and hardiest of American trees, and was prized among Native Americans for the strength and flexibility of bows which were made from its wood.
    IV. The first people to practice agriculture on the American flatlands were faced with an important problem: what would they use to fence their land in a place that was almost entirely without trees or rocks?
    V. Finally, an Illinois farmer brought the settlers a tree that was native to the land between the Red and Arkansas rivers, a tree called the Osage orange.

    The BEST order is:
    A. II, I, V, III, IV   B. I, II, III, IV, V   C. IV, II, V, III, I   D. IV, II, I, III, V

11.____

12. I. After about ten minutes of such spirited and complicated activity, the head dancer is free to make up his or her own movements while maintaining the interest of the New Year's crowd.
    II. The dancer will then perform a series of leg kicks, while at the same time operating the lion's mouth with his own hand and moving the ears and eyes by means of a string which is attached to the dancer's own mouth.
    III. The most difficult role of this dance belongs to the one who controls the lion's head; this person must lead all the other "parts" of the lion through the choreographed segments of the dance.
    IV. The head dancer begins with a complex series of steps. alternately stepping forward with the head raised, and then retreating a few steps while lowering the head, a movement that is intended to create the impression that the lion is keeping a watchful eye for anything evil.
    V. When performing a traditional Chinese New Year's lion dance, several performers must fit themselves inside a large lion costume and work together to enact different parts of the dance.

    The BEST order is:
    A. V, III, IV, II, I   B. III, IV, II, V, I   C. III, I, V, IV, II   D. IV, II, III, V, I

12.____

13.
   I. For many years the shell of the chambered nautilus was treasured in Europe for its beauty and intricacy, but collectors were unaware that they were in possession of the structure that marked a "missing link" in the evolution of marine mollusks.
   II. The nautilus, however, evolved a series of enclosed chambers in its shell, and invented a new use for the structure: the shell began to serve as a buoyancy device.
   III. Equipped with this new flotation device, the nautilus did not need the single, muscular foot of its predecessors, but instead developed flaps, tentacles, and a gentle form of jet propulsion that transformed it into the first mollusk able to take command of its own density and explore a three-dimensional world.
   IV. By pumping and adjusting air pressure into the chambers, the nautilus could spend the day resting on the bottom, and then rise toward the surface at night in search of food.
   V. The nautilus shell looks like a large snail shell, similar to those of its ancestors, who used their shells as protective coverings while they were anchored to the sea floor.
   The BEST order is:
   A. V, II, IV, I, III   B. V, I, II, III, IV   C. I, II, V, III, IV   D. I, V, II, IV, III

14.
   I. While France and England battled for control of the region, the Acadiens prospered on the fertile farmland, which was finally secured by England in 1713.
   II. Early in the 17th century, settlers from Western France founded a colony called Acadie in what is now the Canadian province of Nova Scotia.
   III. At this time, English officials feared the presence of spies among the Acadiens who might be loyal to their French homeland, and the Acadiens were deported to spots along the Atlantic and Caribbean shores of America.
   IV. The French settlers remained on this land, under English rule, for around forty years, until the beginning of the French and Indian War, another conflict between France and England.
   V. As the Acadien refugees drifted toward a final home in Southern Louisiana, neighbors shortened their name to "Cadien," and finally "Cajun," the name which the descendants of early Acadiens still call themselves.
   The BEST order is:
   A. I, IV, II, III, V   B. II, I, III, V, IV   C. II, I, IV, III, V   D. V, II, III, IV, I

15.
   I. Traditional households in the Eastern and Western regions of Africa serve two meals a day—one at around noon, and the other in the evening.
   II. The starch is then used in the way that Americans might use a spoon, to scoop up a portion of the main dish on the person's plate.
   III. The reason for the starch's inclusion in every meal has to do with taste as well as nutrition; African food can be very spicy, and the starch is known to cool the burning effect of the main dish.
   IV. When serving these meals, the main dish is usually served on individual plates, and the starch is served on a communal plate, from which diners break off a piece of bread or scoop rice or fufu in their fingers.

V. The typical meals usually consist of a thick stew or soup as the main course, and an accompanying starch—either bread, rice, or *fufu*, a starchy grain paste similar in consistency to mashed potatoes.

The BEST order is:

A. V, II, III, IV, I B. V, I, IV, III, II C. I, IV, V, III, II D. I, V, IV, II, III

16.
I. In the early days of the American Midwest, Indiana settlers sometimes came together to hold an event called an apple peeling, where neighboring settlers gathered at the homestead of a host family to help prepare the hosts' apple crop for cooking, canning, and making apple butter.
II. At the beginning of the event, each peeler sat down in front of a ten- or twenty-gallon stone jar and was given a crock of apples and a paring knife.
III. Once a peeler had finished with a crock, another was placed next to him; if the peeler was an unmarried man, he kept a strict count of the number of apples he had peeled, because the winner was allowed to kiss the girl of his choice.
IV. The peeling usually ended by 9:30 in the evening, when the neighbors gathered in the host family's parlor for a dance social.
V. The apples were peeled, cored, and quartered, and then placed into the jar.

The BEST order is:

A. I, V, III, IV, II B. II, V, III, IV, I C. I, II, V, III, IV D. II, I, V, IV, III

16.____

17.
I. If your pet turtle is a land turtle and is native to temperate climates, it will stop eating some time in October, which should be your cue to prepare the turtle for hibernation.
II. The box should then be covered with a wire screen, which will protect the turtle from any rodents or predators that might want to take advantage of a motionless and helpless animal.
III. When your turtle hasn't eaten for a while and appears ready to hibernate, it should be moved to its winter quarters, most likely a cellar or garage, where the temperature should range between 40° and 45°F.
IV. Instead of feeding the turtle, you should bathe it every day in warm water, to encourage the turtle to empty its intestines in preparation for its long winter sleep.
V. Here the turtle should be placed in a well-ventilated box whose bottom is covered with a moisture-absorbing layer of clay beads, and then filled three-fourths full with almost dry peat moss or wood chips, into which the turtle will burrow and sleep for several months.

The BEST order is:

A. I, IV, III, V, II B. III, IV, II, V, I C. III, II, IV, I, V D. IV, V, II, III, I

17.____

18.
I. Once he has reached the nest, the hunter uses two sturdy bamboo poles like huge chopsticks to pull the next away from the mountainside, into a large basket that will be lowered to people waiting below.
II. The world's largest honeybees colonize the Nealese mountainsides, building honeycombs as large as a person on sheer rock faces that are often hundreds of feet high.

18.____

III. In the remote mountain country of Nepal, a small band of "honey hunters" carry out a tradition so ancient that 10,000 year-old drawings of the practice have been found in the caves of Nepal.
IV. To harvest the honey and beeswax from these combs, a honey hunter climbs above the nests, lowers a long bamboo-fiber ladder over the cliff, and then climbs down.
V. Throughout this dangerous practice, the hunter is stung repeatedly, and only the veterans, with skin that has been toughened over the years, are able to return from a hunt without the painful swelling caused by stings.

The BEST order is:
A. II, IV, III, V, I   B. II, IV, I, V, III   C. V, III, II, IV, I   D. III, II, IV, I, V

19. I. After the Romans left Britain, there were relentless attacks on the islands from the barbarian tribes of northern Germany—the Angles, Saxons, and Jutes.
II. As the empire weakened, Roman soldiers withdrew from Britain, leaving behind a country that continued to practice the Christian religion that had been introduced by the Romans.
III. Early Latin writings tell of a Christian warrior named Arturius (Arthur, in English) who led the British citizens to defeat these barbarian invades, and brought an extended period of peace to the lands of Britain.
IV. Long ago, the British Isles were part of the far-flung Roman Empire that extended across most of Europe and into Africa and Asia.
V. The romantic legend of King Arthur and his knights of the Round Table, one of the most popular and widespread stories of all time, appears to have some foundation in history.

The BEST order is:
A. V, IV, III, II, I   B. V, IV, II, I, III   C. IV, V, II, III, I   D. IV, III, II, I, V

19.____

20. I. The cylinder was allowed to cool until it could stand on its own, and then it was cut from the tube and split down the side with a single straight cut.
II. Nineteenth-century glassmakers, who had not yet discovered the glazier's modern techniques for making panes of glass, had to create a method for converting their blown gas into flat sheets.
III. The bubble was then pierced at the end to make a hole that opened up while the glassmaker gently spun it, creating a cylinder of glass.
IV. Turned on its side and laid on a conveyor belt, the cylinder was strengthened, or tempered, by being heated again and cooled very slowly, eventually flattening out into a single rectangular of glass.
V. To do this, the glassmaker dipped the end of a long tube into melted glass and blew into the other end of the tube, creating an expanding bubble of glass.

The BEST order is:
A. II, V, III, IV, I   B. II, IV, V, III, I   C. III, V, II, IV, I   D. III, I, IV, V, II

20.____

21. I. The splints are almost always hidden, but horses are occasionally born whose splinted toes project from the leg on either side, just above the hoof.
     II. The second and fourth toes remained, but shrank to thin splints of bone that fused invisibly to the horse's leg bone.
     III. Horses are unique among mammals, having evolved feet that each end in what is essentially a single toe, capped by a large, sturdy hoof.
     IV. Julius Caesar, an emperor of ancient Rome, was said to have owned one of these three-toed horses, and considered it so special that he would not permit anyone else to ride it.
     V. Though the horse's earlier ancestors possessed the traditional mammalian set of five toes on each foot, the horse has retained only its third toe; its first and fifth toes disappeared completely as the horse evolved.
     The BEST order is:
     A. III, V, II, I, IV   B. V, III, II, IV, I   C. III, II, V, I, IV   D. V, II, III, I, IV

22. I. The new building materials—some of which are twenty feet long, and weigh nearly six tons—were transported to Pohnpei on rafts, and were brought into their present position by using hibiscus fiber ropes and leverage to move the stone columns upward along the inclined trunks of coconut palm trees.
     II. The ancestors built great fires to heat the stone, and then poured cool seawater on the columns, which caused the stone to contract and split along natural fracture lines.
     III. The now-abandoned enclave of Nan Madol, a group of 92 man-made islands off the shore of the Micronesian island of Pohnpei, is estimated to have been built around the year 500 A.D.
     IV. The islanders say their ancestors quarried stone columns from a nearby island, where large basalt columns were formed by the cooling of molten lava.
     V. The structures of Nan Madol are remarkable for the sheer size of some of the stone "longs" or columns that were used to create the walls of the offshore community, and today anthropologists can only rely on the information of existing local people for clues about how Nan Madol was built.
     The BEST order is:
     A. V, IV, III, II, I   B. V, III, I, IV, II   C. III, V, IV, II, I   D. III, I, IV, II, V

23. I. One of the most easily manipulated substances on earth, glass can be made into ceramic tiles that are composed of over 90% air.
     II. NASA's space shuttles are the first spacecraft ever designed to leave and re-enter the earth's atmosphere while remaining intact.
     III. These ceramic tiles are such effective insulators that when a tile emerges from the oven in which it was fired, it can be held safely in a person's hand by the edges while its interior still glows at a temperature well over 2000°F.
     IV. Eventually, the engineers were led to a material that is as old as our most ancient civilization.
     V. Because the temperature during atmospheric re-entry is so incredibly hot, it took NASA's engineers some time to find a substance capable of protecting the shuttles.

The BEST order is:
   A. V, II, I, II, IV   B. II, V, IV, I, III   C. II, III, I, IV, V   D. V, IV, III, I, II

24.
  I. The secret to teaching any parakeet to talk is patience, and the understanding that when a bird talks," it is simply imitating what it hears, rather than putting ideas into words.
  II. You should stay just out of sight of the bird and repeat the phrase you want it to learn, for at least fifteen minutes every morning and evening.
  III. It is important to leave the bird without any words of encouragement or farewell; otherwise it might combine stray remarks or phrases, such as "Good night," with the phrase you are trying to teach it.
  IV. For this reason, to train your bird to imitate your words you should keep it free of any distractions, especially other noises, while you are giving it "lesson."
  V. After your repetition, you should quietly leave the bird alone for a while, to think over what it has just heard.

The BEST order is:
   A. I, IV, II, V, III   B. I, II, IV, III, V   C. III, II, I, V, IV   D. III, I, V, IV, II

24.____

25.
  I. As a school approaches, fishermen from neighboring communities join their fishing boats together as a fleet, and string their gill nets together to make a huge fence that is held up by cork floats.
  II. At a signal from the party leaders, or *nakura*, the family members pound the sides of the boats or beat the water with long poles, creating a sudden and deafening noise.
  III. The fishermen work together to drag the trap into a half-circle that may reach 300 yards in diameter, and then the families move their boats to form the other half of the circle around the school of fish.
  IV. The school of fish flee from the commotion into the awaiting trap, where a final wall of net is thrown over the open end of the half-circle, securing the day's haul.
  V. Indonesian people from the area around the Sulu islands live on the sea, in floating villages made of lashed-together or stilted homes, and make much of their living by fishing their home waters for migrating schools of snapper, scad, and other fish.

The BEST order is:
   A. I, V, III, IV, II   B. I, II, IV, III, V   C. V, I, II, III, IV   D. V, I, III, II, IV

25.____

KEY (CORRECT ANSWERS)

1.	D	11.	C
2.	D	12.	A
3.	B	13.	D
4.	A	14.	C
5.	C	15.	D
6.	C	16.	C
7.	D	17.	A
8.	D	18.	D
9.	A	19.	B
10.	B	20.	A

21. A
22. C
23. B
24. A
25. D

PHILOSOPHY, PRINCIPLES, PRACTICES, AND TECHNICS
OF
SUPERVISION, ADMINISTRATION, MANAGEMENT, AND ORGANIZATION

TABLE OF CONTENTS

	Page
MEANING OF SUPERVISION	1
THE OLD AND THE NEW SUPERVISION	1
THE EIGHT (8) BASIC PRINCIPLES OF THE NEW SUPERVISION	1
I. Principle of Responsibility	1
II. Principle of Authority	2
III. Principle of Self-Growth	2
IV. Principle of Individual Worth	2
V. Principle of Creative Leadership	2
VI. Principle of Success and Failure	2
VII. Principle of Science	3
VIII. Principle of Cooperation	3
WHAT IS ADMINISTRATION?	3
I. Practices Commonly Classed as "Supervisory"	3
II. Practices Commonly Classed as "Administrative"	3
III. Practices Commonly Classed as Both "Supervisory" and "Administrative"	4
RESPONSIBILITIES OF THE SUPERVISOR	4
COMPETENCIES OF THE SUPERVISOR	4
THE PROFESSIONAL SUPERVISOR-EMPLOYEE RELATIONSHIP	4
MINI-TEXT IN SUPERVISION, ADMINISTRATION, MANAGEMENT, AND ORGANIZATION	5
I. Brief Highlights	5
A. Levels of Management	6
B. What the Supervisor Must Learn	6
C. A Definition of Supervision	6
D. Elements of the Team Concept	6
E. Principles of Organization	6
F. The Four Important Parts of Every Job	7
G. Principles of Delegation	7
H. Principles of Effective Communications	7
I. Principles of Work Improvement	7
J. Areas of Job Improvement	7
K. Seven Key Points in Making Improvements	8

L.	Corrective Techniques for Job Improvement	8
M.	A Planning Checklist	8
N.	Five Characteristics of Good Directions	9
O.	Types of Directions	9
P.	Controls	9
Q.	Orienting the New Employee	9
R.	Checklist for Orienting New Employees	9
S.	Principles of Learning	10
T.	Causes of Poor Performance	10
U.	Four Major Steps in On-the-Job Instructions	10
V.	Employees Want Five Things	10
W.	Some Don'ts in Regard to Praise	11
X.	How to Gain Your Workers' Confidence	11
Y.	Sources of Employee Problems	11
Z.	The Supervisor's Key to Discipline	11
AA.	Five Important Processes of Management	12
BB.	When the Supervisor Fails to Plan	12
CC.	Fourteen General Principles of Management	12
DD.	Change	12

II. Brief Topical Summaries — 13
    A. Who/What is the Supervisor? — 13
    B. The Sociology of Work — 13
    C. Principles and Practices of Supervision — 14
    D. Dynamic Leadership — 14
    E. Processes for Solving Problems — 15
    F. Training for Results — 15
    G. Health, Safety, and Accident Prevention — 16
    H. Equal Employment Opportunity — 16
    I. Improving Communications — 16
    J. Self-Development — 17
    K. Teaching and Training — 17
        1. The Teaching Process — 17
            a. Preparation — 17
            b. Presentation — 18
            c. Summary — 18
            d. Application — 18
            e. Evaluation — 18
        2. Teaching Methods — 18
            a. Lecture — 18
            b. Discussion — 18
            c. Demonstration — 19
            d. Performance — 19
            e. Which Method to Use — 19

PHILOSOPHY, PRINCIPLES, PRACTICES, AND TECHNICS
OF
SUPERVISION, ADMINISTRATION, MANAGEMENT, AND ORGANIZATION

MEANING OF SUPERVISION

The extension of the democratic philosophy has been accompanied by an extension in the scope of supervision. Modern leaders and supervisors no longer think of supervision in the narrow sense of being confined chiefly to visiting employees, supplying materials, or rating the staff. They regard supervision as being intimately related to all the concerned agencies of society, they speak of the supervisor's function in terms of "growth," rather than the "improvement" of employees.

This modern concept of supervision may be defined as follows: Supervision is leadership and the development of leadership within groups which are cooperatively engaged in inspection, research, training, guidance, and evaluation.

THE OLD AND THE NEW SUPERVISION

TRADITIONAL
1. Inspection
2. Focused on the employee
3. Visitation
4. Random and haphazard
5. Imposed and authoritarian
6. One person usually

MODERN
1. Study and analysis
2. Focused on aims, materials, methods, supervisors, employees, environment
3. Demonstrations, intervisitation, workshops, directed reading, bulletins, etc.
4. Definitely organized and planned (scientific)
5. Cooperative and democratic
6. Many persons involved (creative)

THE EIGHT (8) BASIC PRINCIPLES OF THE NEW SUPERVISION

I. Principle of Responsibility
   Authority to act and responsibility for acting must be joined.
   A. If you give responsibility, give authority.
   B. Define employee duties clearly.
   C. Protect employees from criticism by others.
   D. Recognize the rights as well as obligations of employees.
   E. Achieve the aims of a democratic society insofar as it is possible within the area of your work.
   F. Establish a situation favorable to training and learning.
   G. Accept ultimate responsibility for everything done in your section, unit, office, division, department.
   H. Good administration and good supervision are inseparable.

II. Principle of Authority
The success of the supervisor is measured by the extent to which the power of authority is not used.
   A. Exercise simplicity and informality in supervision
   B. Use the simplest machinery of supervision
   C. If it is good for the organization as a whole, it is probably justified.
   D. Seldom be arbitrary or authoritative.
   E. Do not base your work on the power of position or of personality.
   F. Permit and encourage the free expression of opinions.

III. Principle of Self-Growth
The success of the supervisor is measured by the extent to which, and the speed with which, he is no longer needed.
   A. Base criticism on principles, not on specifics.
   B. Point out higher activities to employees.
   C. Train for self-thinking by employees to meet new situations.
   D. Stimulate initiative, self-reliance, and individual responsibility
   E. Concentrate on stimulating the growth of employees rather than on removing defects.

IV. Principle of Individual Worth
Respect for the individual is a paramount consideration in supervision.
   A. Be human and sympathetic in dealing with employees.
   B. Don't nag about things to be done.
   C. Recognize the individual differences among employees and seek opportunities to permit best expression of each personality.

V. Principle of Creative Leadership
The best supervision is that which is not apparent to the employee.
   A. Stimulate, don't drive employees to creative action.
   B. Emphasize doing good things.
   C. Encourage employees to do what they do best.
   D. Do not be too greatly concerned with details of subject or method.
   E. Do not be concerned exclusively with immediate problems and activities.
   F. Reveal higher activities and make them both desired and maximally possible.
   G. Determine procedures in the light of each situation but see that these are derived from a sound basic philosophy.
   H. Aid, inspire, and lead so as to liberate the creative spirit latent in all good employees.

VI. Principle of Success and Failure
There are no unsuccessful employees, only unsuccessful supervisors who have failed to give proper leadership.
   A. Adapt suggestions to the capacities, attitudes, and prejudices of employees.
   B. Be gradual, be progressive, be persistent.
   C. Help the employee find the general principle; have the employee apply his own problem to the general principle.
   D. Give adequate appreciation for good work and honest effort.
   E. Anticipate employee difficulties and help to prevent them.
   F. Encourage employees to do the desirable things they will do anyway.
   G. Judge your supervision by the results it secures.

VII. Principle of Science
Successful supervision is scientific, objective, and experimental. It is based on facts, not on prejudices.
- A. Be cumulative in results.
- B. Never divorce your suggestions from the goals of training.
- C. Don't be impatient of results.
- D. Keep all matters on a professional, not a personal, level.
- E. Do not be concerned exclusively with immediate problems and activities.
- F. Use objective means of determining achievement and rating where possible.

VIII. Principle of Cooperation
Supervision is a cooperative enterprise between supervisor and employee.
- A. Begin with conditions as they are.
- B. Ask opinions of all involved when formulating policies.
- C. Organization is as good as its weakest link.
- D. Let employees help to determine policies and department programs.
- E. Be approachable and accessible—physically and mentally.
- F. Develop pleasant social relationships.

WHAT IS ADMINISTRATION

Administration is concerned with providing the environment, the material facilities, and the operational procedures that will promote the maximum growth and development of supervisors and employees. (Organization is an aspect and a concomitant of administration.)

There is no sharp line of demarcation between supervision and administration; these functions are intimately interrelated and, often, overlapping. They are complementary activities.

I. Practices Commonly Classed as "Supervisory"
- A. Conducting employees' conferences
- B. Visiting sections, units, offices, divisions, departments
- C. Arranging for demonstrations
- D. Examining plans
- E. Suggesting professional reading
- F. Interpreting bulletins
- G. Recommending in-service training courses
- H. Encouraging experimentation
- I. Appraising employee morale
- J. Providing for intervisitation

II. Practices Commonly Classified as "Administrative"
- A. Management of the office
- B. Arrangement of schedules for extra duties
- C. Assignment of rooms or areas
- D. Distribution of supplies
- E. Keeping records and reports
- F. Care of audio-visual materials
- G. Keeping inventory records
- H. Checking record cards and books

I. Programming special activities
J. Checking on the attendance and punctuality of employees

III. Practices Commonly Classified as Both "Supervisory" and "Administrative"
A. Program construction
B. Testing or evaluating outcomes
C. Personnel accounting
D. Ordering instructional materials

RESPONSIBILITIES OF THE SUPERVISOR

A person employed in a supervisory capacity must constantly be able to improve his own efficiency and ability. He represent the employer to the employees and only continuous self-examination can make him a capable supervisor.

Leadership and training are the supervisor's responsibility. An efficient working unit is one in which the employees work with the supervisor. It is his job to bring out the best in his employees. He must always be relaxed, courteous, and calm in his association with his employees. Their feelings are important, and a harsh attitude does not develop the most efficient employees.

COMPETENCES OF THE SUPERVISOR

I. Complete knowledge of the duties and responsibilities of his position.
II. To be able to organize a job, plan ahead, and carry through.
III. To have self-confidence and initiative.
IV. To be able to handle the unexpected situation and make quick decisions.
V. To be able to properly train subordinates in the positions they are best suited for.
VI. To be able to keep good human relations among his subordinates.
VII. To be able to keep good human relations between his subordinates and himself and to earn their respect and trust.

THE PROFESSIONAL SUPERVISOR-EMPLOYEE RELATIONSHIP

There are two kinds of efficiency: one kind is only apparent and is produced in organizations through the exercise of mere discipline; this is but a simulation of the second, or true, efficiency which springs from spontaneous cooperation. If you are a manager, no matter how great or small your responsibility, it is your job, in the final analysis, to create and develop this involuntary cooperation among the people whom you supervise. For, no matter how powerful a combination of money, machines, and materials a company may have, this is a dead and sterile thing without a team of willing, thinking, and articulate people to guide it.

The following 21 points are presented as indicative of the exemplary basic relationship that should exist between supervisor and employee:

1. Each person wants to be liked and respected by his fellow employee and wants to be treated with consideration and respect by his superior.
2. The most competent employee will make an error. However, in a unit where good relations exist between the supervisor and his employees, tenseness and fear do not exist. Thus, errors are not hidden or covered up, and the efficiency of a unit is not impaired.

3. Subordinates resent rules, regulations, or orders that are unreasonable or unexplained.
4. Subordinates are quick to resent unfairness, harshness, injustices, and favoritism.
5. An employee will accept responsibility if he knows that he will be complimented for a job well done, and not too harshly chastised for failure; that his supervisor will check the cause of the failure, and, if it was the supervisor's fault, he will assume the blame therefore. If it was the employee's fault, his supervisor will explain the correct method or means of handling the responsibility.
6. An employee wants to receive credit for a suggestion he has made, that is used. If a suggestion cannot be used, the employee is entitled to an explanation. The supervisor should not say "no" and close the subject.
7. Fear and worry slow up a worker's ability. Poor working environment can impair his physical and mental health. A good supervisor avoids forceful methods, threats, and arguments to get a job done.
8. A forceful supervisor is able to train his employees individually and as a team, and is able to motivate them in the proper channels.
9. A mature supervisor is able to properly evaluate his subordinates and to keep them happy and satisfied.
10. A sensitive supervisor will never patronize his subordinates.
11. A worthy supervisor will respect his employees' confidences.
12. Definite and clear-cut responsibilities should be assigned to each executive.
13. Responsibility should always be coupled with corresponding authority.
14. No change should be made in the scope or responsibilities of a position without a definite understanding to that effect on the part of all persons concerned.
15. No executive or employee, occupying a single position in the organization, should be subject to definite orders from more than one source.
16. Orders should never be given to subordinates over the head of a responsible executive. Rather than do this, the officer in question should be supplanted.
17. Criticisms of subordinates should, whoever possible, be made privately, and in no case should a subordinate be criticized in the presence of executives or employees of equal or lower rank.
18. No dispute or difference between executives or employees as to authority or responsibilities should be considered too trivial for prompt and careful adjudication.
19. Promotions, wage changes, and disciplinary action should always be approved by the executive immediately superior to the one directly responsible.
20. No executive or employee should ever be required, or expected, to be at the same time an assistant to, and critic of, another.
21. Any executive whose work is subject to regular inspection should, wherever practicable, be given the assistance and facilities necessary to enable him to maintain an independent check of the quality of his work.

MINI-TEXT IN SUPERVISION, ADMINISTRATION, MANAGEMENT, AND ORGANIZATION

I. Brief Highlights

Listed concisely and sequentially are major headings and important data in the field for quick recall and review.

A. Levels of Management
   Any organization of some size has several levels of management. In terms of a ladder, the levels are:

   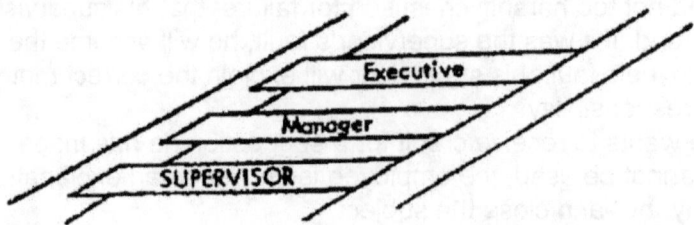

   The first level is very important because it is the beginning point of management leadership.

B. What the Supervisor Must Learn
   A supervisor must learn to:
   1. Deal with people and their differences
   2. Get the job done through people
   3. Recognize the problems when they exist
   4. Overcome obstacles to good performance
   5. Evaluate the performance of people
   6. Check his own performance in terms of accomplishment

C. A Definition of Supervisor
   The term supervisor means any individual having authority, in the interests of the employer, to hire, transfer, suspend, lay-off, recall, promote, discharge, assign, reward, or discipline other employees or responsibility to direct them, or to adjust their grievances, or effectively to recommend such action, if, in connection with the foregoing, exercise of such authority is not of a merely routine or clerical nature but requires the use of independent judgment.

D. Elements of the Team Concept
   What is involved in teamwork? The component parts are:
   1. Members
   2. A leader
   3. Goals
   4. Plans
   5. Cooperation
   6. Spirit

E. Principles of Organization
   1. A team member must know what his job is.
   2. Be sure that the nature and scope of a job are understood.
   3. Authority and responsibility should be carefully spelled out.
   4. A supervisor should be permitted to make the maximum number of decisions affecting his employees.
   5. Employees should report to only one supervisor.
   6. A supervisor should direct only as many employees as he can handle effectively.
   7. An organization plan should be flexible.

8. Inspection and performance of work should be separate.
9. Organizational problems should receive immediate attention.
10. Assign work in line with ability and experience.

F. The Four Important Parts of Every Job
1. Inherent in every job is the *accountability* for results.
2. A second set of factors in every job is *responsibilities*.
3. Along with duties and responsibilities one must have the *authority* to act within certain limits without obtaining permission to proceed.
4. No job exists in a vacuum. The supervisor is surrounded by key *relationships*.

G. Principles of Delegation
Where work is delegated for the first time, the supervisor should think in terms of these questions:
1. Who is best qualified to do this?
2. Can an employee improve his abilities by doing this?
3. How long should an employee spend on this?
4. Are there any special problems for which he will need guidance?
5. How broad a delegation can I make?

H. Principles of Effective Communications
1. Determine the media.
2. To whom directed?
3. Identification and source authority.
4. Is communication understood?

I. Principles of Work Improvement
1. Most people usually do only the work which is assigned to them.
2. Workers are likely to fit assigned work into the time available to perform it.
3. A good workload usually stimulates output.
4. People usually do their best work when they know that results will be reviewed or inspected.
5. Employees usually feel that someone else is responsible for conditions of work, workplace layout, job methods, type of tools/equipment, and other such factors.
6. Employees are usually defensive about their job security.
7. Employees have natural resistance to change.
8. Employees can support or destroy a supervisor.
9. A supervisor usually earns the respect of his people through his personal example of diligence and efficiency.

J. Areas of Job Improvement
The areas of job improvement are quite numerous, but the most common ones which a supervisor can identify and utilize are:
1. Departmental layout
2. Flow of work
3. Workplace layout
4. Utilization of manpower
5. Work methods
6. Materials handling

7. Utilization
8. Motion economy

K. Seven Key Points in Making Improvements
1. Select the job to be improved
2. Study how it is being done now
3. Question the present method
4. Determine actions to be taken
5. Chart proposed method
6. Get approval and apply
7. Solicit worker participation

I. Corrective Techniques of Job Improvement
Specific Problems
1. Size of workload
2. Inability to meet schedules
3. Strain and fatigue
4. Improper use of men and skills
5. Waste, poor quality, unsafe conditions
6. Bottleneck conditions that hinder output
7. Poor utilization of equipment and machine
8. Efficiency and productivity of labor

General Improvement
1. Departmental layout
2. Flow of work
3. Work plan layout
4. Utilization of manpower
5. Work methods
6. Materials handling
7. Utilization of equipment
8. Motion economy

Corrective Techniques
1. Study with scale model
2. Flow chart study
3. Motion analysis
4. Comparison of units produced to standard allowance
5. Methods analysis
6. Flow chart and equipment study
7. Down time vs. running time
8. Motion analysis

M. A Planning Checklist
1. Objectives
2. Controls
3. Delegations
4. Communications
5. Resources
6. Manpower

7. Equipment
8. Supplies and materials
9. Utilization of time
10. Safety
11. Money
12. Work
13. Timing of improvements

N. Five Characteristics of Good Directions
In order to get results, directions must be:
1. Possible of accomplishment
2. Agreeable with worker interests
3. Related to mission
4. Planned and complete
5. Unmistakably clear

O. Types of Directions
1. Demands or direct orders
2. Requests
3. Suggestion or implication
4. volunteering

P. Controls
A typical listing of the overall areas in which the supervisor should establish controls might be:
1. Manpower
2. Materials
3. Quality of work
4. Quantity of work
5. Time
6. Space
7. Money
8. Methods

Q. Orienting the New Employee
1. Prepare for him
2. Welcome the new employee
3. Orientation for the job
4. Follow-up

R. Checklist for Orienting New Employees   Yes   No
1. Do you appreciate the feelings of new employees
   when they first report for work?   ___   ___
2. Are you aware of the fact that the new employee must
   make a big adjustment to his job?   ___   ___
3. Have you given him good reasons for liking the job and
   the organization?   ___   ___
4. Have you prepared for his first day on the job? ___   ___
5. Did you welcome him cordially and make him feel needed? ___ ___

			Yes	No
	6.	Did you establish rapport with him so that he feels free to talk and discuss matters with you?	___	___
	7.	Did you explain his job to him and his relationship to you?	___	___
	8.	Does he know that his work will be evaluated periodically on a basis that is fair and objective?	___	___
	9.	Did you introduce him to his fellow workers in such a way that they are likely to accept him?	___	___
	10.	Does he know what employee benefits he will receive?	___	___
	11.	Does he understand the importance of being on the job and what to do if he must leave his duty station?	___	___
	12.	Has he been impressed with the importance of accident prevention and safe practice?	___	___
	13.	Does he generally know his way around the department?	___	___
	14.	Is he under the guidance of a sponsor who will teach the right way of doing things?	___	___
	15.	Do you plan to follow-up so that he will continue to adjust successfully to his job?	___	___

S. Principles of Learning
   1. Motivation
   2. Demonstration or explanation
   3. Practice

T. Causes of Poor Performance
   1. Improper training for job
   2. Wrong tools
   3. Inadequate directions
   4. Lack of supervisory follow-up
   5. Poor communications
   6. Lack of standards of performance
   7. Wrong work habits
   8. Low morale
   9. Other

U. Four Major Steps in On-The-Job Instruction
   1. Prepare the worker
   2. Present the operation
   3. Tryout performance
   4. Follow-up

V. Employees Want Five Things
   1. Security
   2. Opportunity
   3. Recognition
   4. Inclusion
   5. Expression

11

W. Some Don'ts in Regard to Praise
1. Don't praise a person for something he hasn't done.
2. Don't praise a person unless you can be sincere.
3. Don't be sparing in praise just because your superior withholds it from you.
4. Don't let too much time elapse between good performance and recognition of it

X. How to Gain Your Workers' Confidence
Methods of developing confidence include such things as:
1. Knowing the interests, habits, hobbies of employees
2. Admitting your own inadequacies
3. Sharing and telling of confidence in others
4. Supporting people when they are in trouble
5. Delegating matters that can be well handled
6. Being frank and straightforward about problems and working conditions
7. Encouraging others to bring their problems to you
8. Taking action on problems which impede worker progress

Y. Sources of Employee Problems
On-the-job causes might be such things as:
1. A feeling that favoritism is exercised in assignments
2. Assignment of overtime
3. An undue amount of supervision
4. Changing methods or systems
5. Stealing of ideas or trade secrets
6. Lack of interest in job
7. Threat of reduction in force
8. Ignorance or lack of communications
9. Poor equipment
10. Lack of knowing how supervisor feels toward employee
11. Shift assignments

Off-the-job problems might have to do with:
1. Health
2. Finances
3. Housing
4. Family

Z. The Supervisor's Key to Discipline
There are several key points about discipline which the supervisor should keep in mind:
1. Job discipline is one of the disciplines of life and is directed by the supervisor.
2. It is more important to correct an employee fault than to fix blame for it.
3. Employee performance is affected by problems both on the job and off.
4. Sudden or abrupt changes in behavior can be indications of important employee problems.
5. Problems should be dealt with as soon as possible after they are identified.
6. The attitude of the supervisor may have more to do with solving problems than the techniques of problem solving.
7. Correction of employee behavior should be resorted to only after the supervisor is sure that training or counseling will not be helpful.

8. Be sure to document your disciplinary actions.
9. Make sure that you are disciplining on the basis of facts rather than personal feelings.
10. Take each disciplinary step in order, being careful not to make snap judgments, or decisions based on impatience.

AA. Five Important Processes of Management
1. Planning
2. Organizing
3. Scheduling
4. Controlling
5. Motivating

BB. When the Supervisor Fails to Plan
1. Supervisor creates impression of not knowing his job
2. May lead to excessive overtime
3. Job runs itself—supervisor lacks control
4. Deadlines and appointments missed
5. Parts of the work go undone
6. Work interrupted by emergencies
7. Sets a bad example
8. Uneven workload creates peaks and valleys
9. Too much time on minor details at expense of more important tasks

CC. Fourteen General Principles of Management
1. Division of work
2. Authority and responsibility
3. Discipline
4. Unity of command
5. Unity of direction
6. Subordination of individual interest to general interest
7. Remuneration of personnel
8. Centralization
9. Scalar chain
10. Order
11. Equity
12. Stability of tenure of personnel
13. Initiative
14. Esprit de corps

DD. Change

Bringing about change is perhaps attempted more often, and yet less well understood, than anything else the supervisor does. How do people generally react to change? (People tend to resist change that is imposed upon them by other individuals or circumstances.

Change is characteristic of every situation. It is a part of every real endeavor where the efforts of people are concerned.

1. Why do people resist change?
   People may resist change because of:
   a. Fear of the unknown
   b. Implied criticism
   c. Unpleasant experiences in the past
   d. Fear of loss of status
   e. Threat to the ego
   f. Fear of loss of economic stability

2. How can we best overcome the resistance to change?
   In initiating change, take these steps:
   a. Get ready to sell
   b. Identify sources of help
   c. Anticipate objections
   d. Sell benefits
   e. Listen in depth
   f. Follow up

II. Brief Topical Summaries

   A. Who/What is the Supervisor?
      1. The supervisor is often called the "highest level employee and the lowest level manager."
      2. A supervisor is a member of both management and the work group. He acts as a bridge between the two.
      3. Most problems in supervision are in the area of human relations, or people problems.
      4. Employees expect: Respect, opportunity to learn and to advance, and a sense of belonging, and so forth.
      5. Supervisors are responsible for directing people and organizing work. Planning is of paramount importance.
      6. A position description is a set of duties and responsibilities inherent to a given position.
      7. It is important to keep the position description up-to-date and to provide each employee with his own copy.

   B. The Sociology of Work
      1. People are alike in many ways; however, each individual is unique.
      2. The supervisor is challenged in getting to know employee differences. Acquiring skills in evaluating individuals is an asset.
      3. Maintaining meaningful working relationships in the organization is of great importance.
      4. The supervisor has an obligation to help individuals to develop to their fullest potential.
      5. Job rotation on a planned basis helps to build versatility and to maintain interest and enthusiasm in work groups.
      6. Cross training (job rotation) provides backup skills.

7. The supervisor can help reduce tension by maintaining a sense of humor, providing guidance to employees, and by making reasonable and timely decisions. Employees respond favorably to working under reasonably predictable circumstances.
8. Change is characteristic of all managerial behavior. The supervisor must adjust to changes in procedures, new methods, technological changes, and to a number of new and sometimes challenging situations.
9. To overcome the natural tendency for people to resist change, the supervisor should become more skillful in initiating change.

C. Principles and Practices of Supervision
1. Employees should be required to answer to only one superior.
2. A supervisor can effectively direct only a limited number of employees, depending upon the complexity, variety, and proximity of the jobs involved.
3. The organizational chart presents the organization in graphic form. It reflects lines of authority and responsibility as well as interrelationships of units within the organization.
4. Distribution of work can be improved through an analysis using the "Work Distribution Chart."
5. The "Work Distribution Chart" reflects the division of work within a unit in understandable form.
6. When related tasks are given to an employee, he has a better chance of increasing his skills through training.
7. The individual who is given the responsibility for tasks must also be given the appropriate authority to insure adequate results.
8. The supervisor should delegate repetitive, routine work. Preparation of recurring reports, maintaining leave and attendance records are some examples.
9. Good discipline is essential to good task performance. Discipline is reflected in the actions of employees on the job in the absence of supervision.
10. Disciplinary action may have to be taken when the positive aspects of discipline have failed. Reprimand, warning, and suspension are examples of disciplinary action.
11. If a situation calls for a reprimand, be sure it is deserved and remember it is to be done in private.

D. Dynamic Leadership
1. A style is a personal method or manner of exerting influence.
2. Authoritarian leaders often see themselves as the source of power and authority.
3. The democratic leader often perceives the group as the source of authority and power.
4. Supervisors tend to do better when using the pattern of leadership that is most natural for them.
5. Social scientists suggest that the effective supervisor use the leadership style that best fits the problem or circumstances involved.
6. All four styles—telling, selling, consulting, joining—have their place. Using one does not preclude using the other at another time.

7. The theory X point of view assumes that the average person dislikes work, will avoid it whenever possible, and must be coerced to achieve organizational objectives.
8. The theory Y point of view assumes that the average person considers work to be a natural as play, and, when the individual is committed, he requires little supervision or direction to accomplish desired objectives.
9. The leader's basic assumptions concerning human behavior and human nature affect his actions, decisions, and other managerial practices.
10. Dissatisfaction among employees is often present, but difficult to isolate. The supervisor should seek to weaken dissatisfaction by keeping promises, being sincere and considerate, keeping employees informed, and so forth.
11. Constructive suggestions should be encouraged during the natural progress of the work.

E. Processes for Solving Problems
1. People find their daily tasks more meaningful and satisfying when they can improve them.
2. The causes of problems, or the key factors, are often hidden in the background. Ability to solve problems often involves the ability to isolate them from their backgrounds. There is some substance to the cliché that some persons "can't see the forest for the trees."
3. New procedures are often developed from old ones. Problems should be broken down into manageable parts. New ideas can be adapted from old one.
4. People think differently in problem-solving situations. Using a logical, patterned approach is often useful. One approach found to be useful includes these steps:
   a. Define the problem
   b. Establish objectives
   c. Get the facts
   d. Weigh and decide
   e. Take action
   f. Evaluate action

F. Training for Results
1. Participants respond best when they feel training is important to them.
2. The supervisor has responsibility for the training and development of those who report to him.
3. When training is delegated to others, great care must be exercised to insure the trainer has knowledge, aptitude, and interest for his work as a trainer.
4. Training (learning) of some type goes on continually. The most successful supervisor makes certain the learning contributes in a productive manner to operational goals.
5. New employees are particularly susceptible to training. Older employees facing new job situations require specific training, as well as having need for development and growth opportunities.
6. Training needs require continuous monitoring.
7. The training officer of an agency is a professional with a responsibility to assist supervisors in solving training problems.

8. Many of the self-development steps important to the supervisor's own growth are equally important to the development of peers and subordinates. Knowledge of these is important when the supervisor consults with others on development and growth opportunities.

G. Health, Safety, and Accident Prevention
1. Management-minded supervisors take appropriate measures to assist employees in maintaining health and in assuring safe practices in the work environment.
2. Effective safety training and practices help to avoid injury and accidents.
3. Safety should be a management goal. All infractions of safety which are observed should be corrected without exception.
4. Employees' safety attitude, training and instruction, provision of safe tools and equipment, supervision, and leadership are considered highly important factors which contribute to safety and which can be influenced directly by supervisors.
5. When accidents do occur, they should be investigated promptly for very important reasons, including the fact that information which is gained can be used to prevent accidents in the future.

H. Equal Employment Opportunity
1. The supervisor should endeavor to treat all employees fairly, without regard to religion, race, sex, or national origin.
2. Groups tend to reflect the attitude of the leader. Prejudice can be detected even in very subtle form. Supervisors must strive to create a feeling of mutual respect and confidence in every employee.
3. Complete utilization of all human resources is a national goal. Equitable consideration should be accorded women in the work force, minority-group members, the physically and mentally handicapped, and the older employee. The important question is: "Who can do the job?"
4. Training opportunities, recognition for performance, overtime assignments, promotional opportunities, and all other personnel actions are to be handled on an equitable basis.

I. Improving Communications
1. Communications is achieving understanding between the sender and the receiver of a message. It also means sharing information—the creation of understanding.
2. Communication is basic to all human activity. Words are means of conveying meanings; however, real meanings are in people.
3. There are very practical differences in the effectiveness of one-way, impersonal, and two-way communications. Words spoken face-to-face are better understood. Telephone conversations are effective, but lack the rapport of person-to-person exchanges. The whole person communicates.
4. Cooperation and communication in an organization go hand in hand. When there is a mutual respect between people, spelling out rules and procedures for communicating is unnecessary.
5. There are several barriers to effective communications. These include failure to listen with respect and understanding, lack of skill in feedback, and misinterpreting the meanings of words used by the speaker. It is also common

practice to listen to what we want to hear, and tune out things we do not want to hear.
6. Communication is management's chief problem. The supervisor should accept the challenge to communicate more effectively and to improve interagency and intra-agency communications.
7. The supervisor may often plan for and conduct meetings. The planning phase is critical and may determine the success or the failure of a meeting.
8. Speaking before groups usually requires extra effort. Stage fright may never disappear completely, but it can be controlled.

J. Self-Development
1. Every employee is responsible for his own self-development.
2. Toastmaster and toastmistress clubs offer opportunities to improve skills in oral communications.
3. Planning for one's own self-development is of vital importance. Supervisors know their own strengths and limitations better than anyone else.
4. Many opportunities are open to aid the supervisor in his developmental efforts, including job assignments; training opportunities, both governmental and non-governmental—to include universities and professional conferences and seminars.
5. Programmed instruction offers a means of studying at one's own rate.
6. Where difficulties may arise from a supervisor's being away from his work for training, he may participate in televised home study or correspondence courses to meet his self-development needs.

K. Teaching and Training
1. The Teaching Process
Teaching is encouraging and guiding the learning activities of students toward established goals. In most cases this process consists of five steps: preparation, presentation, summarization, evaluation, and application.

 a. Preparation
 Preparation is two-fold in nature; that of the supervisor and the employee. Preparation by the supervisor is absolutely essential to success. He must know what, when, where, how, and whom he will teach. Some of the factors that should be considered are:
 1) The objectives
 2) The materials needed
 3) The methods to be used
 4) Employee participation
 5) Employee interest
 6) Training aids
 7) Evaluation
 8) Summarization

 Employee preparation consists in preparing the employee to receive the material. Probably the most important single factor in the preparation of the employee is arousing and maintaining his interest. He must know the objectives of the training, why he is there, how the material can be used, and its importance to him.

b. Presentation
In presentation, have a carefully designed plan and follow it. The plan should be accurate and complete, yet flexible enough to meet situations as they arise. The method of presentation will be determined by the particular situation and objectives.

c. Summary
A summary should be made at the end of every training unit and program. In addition, there may be internal summaries depending on the nature of the material being taught. The important thing is that the trainee must always be able to understand how each part of the new material relates to the whole.

d. Application
The supervisor must arrange work so the employee will be given a chance to apply new knowledge or skills while the material is still clear in his mind and interest is high. The trainee does not really know whether he has learned the material until he has been given a chance to apply it. If the material is not applied, it loses most of its value.

e. Evaluation
The purpose of all training is to promote learning. To determine whether the training has been a success or failure, the supervisor must evaluate this learning.
In the broadest sense, evaluation includes all the devices, methods, skills, and techniques used by the supervisor to keep himself and the employees informed as to their progress toward the objectives they are pursuing. The extent to which the employee has mastered the knowledge, skills, and abilities, or changed his attitudes, as determined by the program objectives, is the extent to which instruction has succeeded or failed.
Evaluation should not be confined to the end of the lesson, day, or program but should be used continuously. We shall note later the way this relates to the rest of the teaching process.

2. Teaching Methods
A teaching method is a pattern of identifiable student and instructor activity used in presenting training material.
All supervisors are faced with the problem of deciding which method should be used at a given time.

a. Lecture
The lecture is direct oral presentation of material by the supervisor. The present trend is to place less emphasis on the trainer's activity and more on that of the trainee.

b. Discussion
Teaching by discussion or conference involves using questions and other techniques to arouse interest and focus attention upon certain areas, and by doing so creating a learning situation. This can be one of the most

valuable methods because it gives the employees an opportunity to express their ideas and pool their knowledge.

c. Demonstration
The demonstration is used to teach how something works or how to do something. It can be used to show a principle or what the results of a series of actions will be. A well-staged demonstration is particularly effective because it shows proper methods of performance in a realistic manner.

d. Performance
Performance is one of the most fundamental of all learning techniques or teaching methods. The trainee may be able to tell how a specific operation should be performed but he cannot be sure he knows how to perform the operation until he has done so.
As with all methods, there are certain advantages and disadvantages to each method.

e. Which Method to Use
Moreover, there are other methods and techniques of teaching. It is difficult to use any method without other methods entering into it. In any learning situation, a combination of methods is usually more effective than any one method alone.

Finally, evaluation must be integrated into the other aspects of the teaching-learning process.

It must be used in the motivation of the trainees; it must be used to assist in developing understanding during the training; and it must be related to employee application of the results of training.

This is distinctly the role of the supervisor.

---

www.ingramcontent.com/pod-product-compliance
Lightning Source LLC
Chambersburg PA
CBHW081819300426
44116CB00014B/2420